Mini
amigurumi

62 CROCHET MINI AMIGURUMI TOYS

VIVIKA VAINA

The Wandering Deer

Tuva Publishing
www.tuvapublishing.com

Address Merkez Mah. Cavusbasi Cad. No71
Cekmekoy - Istanbul 34782 / Türkiye
Tel +9 0216 642 62 62

Mini Amigurumi

First Print August 2024

All Global Copyrights Belong to
Tuva Tekstil ve Yayıncılık Ltd.

Content Crochet

Editor in Chief Ayhan DEMİRPEHLİVAN

Project Editor Kader DEMİRPEHLİVAN

Designers Vivika VAINA

Technical Editor Leyla ARAS

Graphic Designers Ömer ALP, Abdullah BAYRAKÇI,
Tarık TOKGÖZ, Yunus GÜLDOĞAN

Photography Tuva Publishing

Crochet Tech Editor Megan BARCLAY

ISBN 978-605-7834-77-5

 TuvaYayincilik    TuvaPublishing

 TuvaYayincilik    TuvaPublishing

INTRODUCTION

Welcome to the wonderful world of amigurumi! In this book, you'll find six adorable scenes to crochet, along with many more cute amigurumi projects that you can make in one sitting!

Picture celebrating birthdays, discovering nature's creatures, caring for plants, and exploring the world - there's a little story waiting to be told with every stitch.

Choose colors that make your heart sing and make these mini dolls uniquely yours. After all, crocheting amigurumi is all about having fun and letting your imagination run wild!

As a child, I loved a book about a girl who fixed dolls and plushies. Little did I know that almost three decades later, I'd find myself sewing eyes and attaching arms and legs to my own tiny creations. It's something I've always loved doing.

I've tried many crafts over the years, from drawing to sewing, but crochet has always held a special place in my heart. Designing amigurumi allows me to tell stories, create scenes, and add special touches to each piece - all with a touch of love.

This book is a dream come true for me. It's filled with patterns that I've designed with love and care, and I hope they bring you as much joy as they've brought me. I'm grateful to my friends Cressida, Jessica, Sandy, and Tanya, who've helped me along the way. Their support, encouragement, patience, and hard work to test every pattern within these pages means the world to me. And to my beloved family, thank you for your unwavering support and understanding as I embarked on this creative journey.

So, I invite you to dive into these pages and let your imagination run wild.

Happy crocheting!

Love, Vivika

Project Gallery

P.18

P.32

P.50

P.66

P.78

P.88

P.94

P.102

P.114

INTRODUCTION
P.3

PROJECT GALLERY
P.4

BASICS & TECHNIQUES
P.6

MATERIALS
P.17

CROCHET
BASICS & TECHNIQUES

SAFETY WARNING & GENERAL SAFETY TIPS

Safety Warning

When making toys for children under the age of three (including babies), be sure to use child-friendly products.

We advise you avoid the following:

• 'Fuzzy' yarns, where the lint can be inhaled or swallowed.
• Glass eyes or beads, which can shatter or break.
• Small beads and buttons (including some safety eyes), which can be chewed off and swallowed or become a choking hazard.

General Safety Tips

1 Make sure each piece of the toy is sewn firmly onto the body.

2 Instead of using safety eyes, buttons or beads, you can use crocheted or felt circles, sewn on firmly.

3 You can create features on your toys with simple embroidery stitches.

Note: These safety warnings also apply when you make toys for pets.

GENERAL INFORMATION FOR MAKING AMIGURUMI

Choosing a Hook Size

Use a hook which is a size or two smaller than what is recommended on the yarn label. The fabric created should be tight enough so that the stuffing does not show through the stitches.

Right Side vs Wrong Side of the Fabric

It is important to be able to distinguish between the 'right' (front) and 'wrong' (back) side of the crocheted fabric.

Right Side

Wrong Side

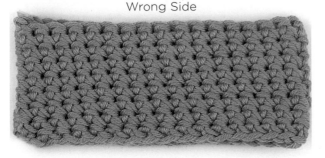

When working in a spiral or joined round, the right side of the fabric is always facing you. (see "Right Side" image). When working in rows or turned rounds, the lines within the fabric alternate between the 'right' and 'wrong' side (see "Single Crochet Rows" image below).

Single Crochet Rows

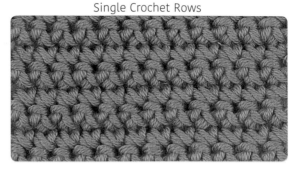

Working in a Spiral

Most of the amigurumi pieces are worked in a continuous spiral to create the three dimensional shapes needed. Working in a spiral means that at the end of a round, you do not join (or close) with a slip stitch into the first stitch of the round. When you get to the end of the round, you start the next round by just working a stitch into the next stitch (which is the first stitch of the previous round).

Working in Joined (Closed) Rounds

Some parts of an amigurumi pattern might have 'joined rounds'. This is where, at the end of the round, you join with a slip stitch in the first stitch of the round. The next round starts with a number of chain stitches (based on the height of the stitches used), and then you continue working stitches for the next round.

Note: Do not turn at the end of each joined round, unless instructed to do so.

Working in Rows

For some accessories or patches for your amigurumi, you will need to work in rows. Each row starts by turning the piece and working some chain stitches (known as the 'turning chain'). The number of chain stitches worked is based on the height of the stitches used.

Stuffing

Amigurumi need a lot of stuffing. The best material to stuff an amigurumi with is polyester fiberfill stuffing specifically designed for soft toys. Using a chopstick can help you fill tiny pieces.

But how do you determine what is the right amount of stuffing? You want a firm and sturdy amigurumi; if it is really soft and loses its shape, then it means it is understuffed. Is there such a thing as too much stuffing? Definitely. When tension creates holes in your piece and the stuffing is visible, or if the shape of the piece is distorted, it means your amigurumi is overstuffed.

When is the right time to stuff? Do we need to stuff all the pieces? In all the patterns of this book, you will find instructions on when and whether you need to stuff a piece.

Using Stitch Markers

When working in a spiral (continuous rounds), it is very important to keep track of the beginning of the round with a stitch marker, otherwise you don't know where one round ends and another begins. You can use the plastic markers specifically designed for this purpose, or opt for a piece of yarn or even a paperclip. Personally, I prefer to use the yarn end from the magic ring (or the original slipknot), to mark the start of my round. It is always readily available and impossible to lose, as it is attached to the piece already.

ADAPTING THE DESIGN

There are many ways you can make your amigurumi toy personalised.

Size By choosing a different weight yarn, you can make your toys either bigger (using thicker yarn) or smaller (using thinner yarn or thread). Remember to change your hook size, too.

Colors This is the easiest way to make your toy personalised. Select colors to match décor or personal preference.

Characteristics Changing the facial features of toys gives them a whole new character. Adding (or removing) embellishments can change the overall look of a toy.

Eyes Just by changing the size or color of the eyes, you can create a totally different facial expression. Instead of using safety eyes, you can use buttons or beads for eyes. If there is a safety concern, you can sew on small bits of felt for eyes or embroider the features.

Applique Patches Whether they are crocheted, fabric or felt (or a combination of these), adding appliqué patches to your toy is a great way to make them distinctive. They can be facial features, such as eyes, noses, mouths, cheeks, and maybe even ears. You can also make novelty appliqué patches to use as embellishments on the toys. For example – flowers on a dress, an eye-patch for a pirate, an overall patch for a farmer. The creativity becomes endless.

Embroidery By adding embroidery stitches to the face, the character of the toy can change. Whether you use plain embroidery stitches (straight stitch, back stitch, etc.) or fancy ones (satin stitch, French knot, bullion stitch, etc.), your toy will take on a personality of its own. You can also use the cross-stitch technique to create a personalised look.

Note: Embroider all facial features to make a child-safe toy.

Adding Accessories To create your one-of-a-kind toy, you can add various decorations to them. Colored buttons can be used in a variety of ways to spice things up. Using small ribbons and bows can dress up dolls. Attaching a small bunch of flowers or small basket to a doll's hand tells a new story.

However you choose to give your toy character, each one ends up being distingué!

Blusher

Adding some color to the cheeks is another way of changing the character of toys. I always embroider two pink stitches under each eye as cheeks. Another way to add cheeks is by applying a cosmetic pink blusher or eyeshadow using a small makeup brush or cotton bud (Q-Tip). You could also rub a red pencil on a piece of fabric, pressing down hard, then rub the 'red' fabric on the cheeks as a blusher.

CROCHET TERMINOLOGY

This book uses US crochet terminology.

Basic conversion chart

US	UK
slip stitch (**sl st**)	slip stitch (**sl st**)
chain (**ch**)	chain (**ch**)
single crochet (**sc**)	double crochet (**dc**)
double crochet (**dc**)	treble crochet (**tr**)
half-double crochet (**hdc**)	half treble (**htr**)
treble (triple) crochet (**tr**)	double treble (**dtr**)

Abbreviations Of The Basic Stitches

ch	Chain Stitch
sl st	Slip Stitch
sc	Single Crochet Stitch
hdc	Half-Double Crochet Stitch
dc	Double Crochet Stitch
st(s)	Stitch(es)

Concise Action Terms

dec	Decrease (single crochet the next two stitches together)
inc	Increase (work two single crochet stitches into the same stitch)
dc-inc	Double crochet increase (work two double crochet stitches into the same stitch)
join	Join two stitches together to complete the end of a round (usually a sl st) or attach two pieces together (usually a sc), or join a new ball/color of yarn to a piece with a sl st, slip knot or sc
turn	Turn your crochet piece so you can work back for the next row/round
yo	Yarn over the hook (either to pull up a loop or to draw through the loops on the hook)

Standard Symbols Used in Patterns

[ ]	Work the instructions within the brackets as many times as directed
( )	Work the instructions within the parentheses in the same stitch or space indicated

CROCHET BASICS

Slip Knot

Almost every crochet project starts with a slip knot on the hook. This is not mentioned in any pattern – it is assumed.

To make a slip knot, form a loop with your yarn (the tail end hanging behind your loop), insert the hook through the loop and pick up the ball end of the yarn, drawing it through the loop. Keeping the loop on the hook, gently tug the tail end to tighten the knot. Tugging the ball end tightens the loop.

Yarn Over (yo)

This is a common practice, especially with the taller stitches. With a loop on your hook, wrap the yarn (attached to the ball) from back to front around the shaft of your hook.

Chain Stitch (ch)

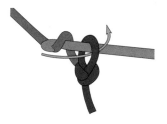

The chain stitch is the foundation of most crochet projects. The foundation chain is a series of chain stitches into which you work the first row of stitches.

To make a chain stitch, start with a slip knot (or loop) on the hook. Yarn over and pull the yarn through the loop on your hook (first chain stitch made). For more chain stitches, repeat: yarn over, pull through loop on hook.

Hint: Don't pull the stitches too tight, otherwise they will be difficult to work into. When counting chain stitches, do not count the slip knot, nor the loop on the hook. Only count the number of 'v's.

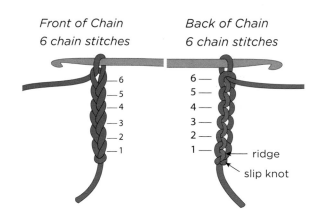

Front of Chain
6 chain stitches

Back of Chain
6 chain stitches

Slip Stitch (sl st)

Starting with a loop on your hook, insert your hook into the stitch or space specified and pull up a loop, pulling it through the loop on your hook as well.

The slip stitch is commonly used to join rounds (join with sl st).

Single Crochet (sc)

Starting with a loop on your hook, insert your hook into the stitch or space specified and pull up a loop (two loops on hook). Yarn over and pull the yarn through both the loops on your hook (first sc made).

The height of a single crochet stitch is one chain high.

When working single crochet stitches into a foundation chain, begin by making the first single crochet into the second chain from the hook. The skipped chain stitch provides the height of the stitch.

At the beginning of a single crochet row or round (except when working in a spiral), start by making one chain stitch (to get the height), then work the first single crochet stitch into the first stitch.

Note: The one chain stitch is never counted as a single crochet stitch.

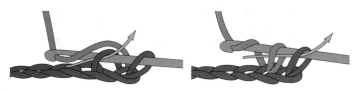

Half-Double Crochet (hdc)

Starting with a loop on your hook, yarn over before inserting your hook into the stitch or space specified and pull up a loop (three loops on hook). Yarn over and pull the yarn through all three loops (first hdc made).

The height of a half-double crochet stitch is two chains high.

When working half-double crochet stitches into a foundation chain, begin the first stitch in the third chain from the hook. The two skipped chains provide the height.

When starting a row or round with a half-double crochet stitch, make two chain stitches and work into the first stitch.

Note: The two chain stitches are never counted as a half-double crochet stitch.

Double Crochet (dc)

Starting with a loop on your hook, yarn over before inserting your hook into the stitch or space specified and pull up a loop (three loops on hook). Yarn over and pull the yarn through two loops (two loops remain on hook). Yarn over and pull the yarn through the remaining two loops on the hook (first dc made).

The height of a double crochet stitch is three chains high.

When working double crochet stitches into a foundation chain, begin the first stitch in the fourth chain from the hook. The three skipped chains count as the first double crochet stitch.

When starting a row or round with a double crochet stitch, make three chain stitches (which count as the first double crochet), skip the first stitch (under the chains) and work a double crochet in the next (second) stitch. On the following row or round, you will be working into the top chain (3rd chain stitch of the three chains) for the first stitch.

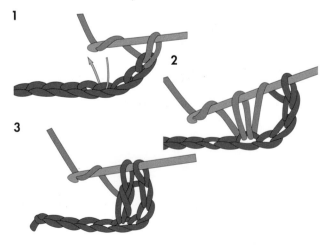

Decrease (dec)

There are two ways to decrease: a normal decrease, and an invisible decrease. The invisible decrease gives a neater result; however, if you find it challenging in certain cases, you can use the normal decrease.

Invisible decrease

Insert your hook into the front loop of each of the next 2 stitches (three loops on hook). *(photos 1-2)*

Yarn over and pull the yarn through the first two loops on the hook (two loops on hook). *(photo 3)*

Yarn over and pull the yarn through both loops on the hook. *(photo 4)*

Normal decrease

Insert your hook into the next stitch and pull up a loop (two loops on hook). *(photo 1)*

Insert your hook into the next stitch and pull up a loop (three loops on hook). *(photo 2)*

Yarn over and draw through all three loops on the hook. *(photo 3)*

Hint: Use the invisible decrease when working in continuous spiral rounds and use the normal decrease when working in rows.

Increase (inc)

Work two single crochet stitches into the same stitch.

Double Crochet Increase (dc-inc)

Work two double crochet stitches into the same stitch.

Changing Colors / Attaching New Yarn

With the current color, work the last stitch before the color change up to the last step of the stitch (the last yarn over). Using the new color, yarn over and pull the new color through the remaining loops on the hook.

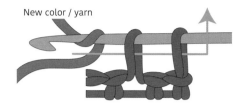

New color / yarn

Sewing Closed

Working into the front loops of the last round, thread your needle from the inside to the outside for each stitch around. *(photo 1)*

Pull the yarn gently to close the hole. Once the opening is closed, insert your needle back through the center of the closed hole and bring it out to an inconspicuous place on the piece. *(photo 2)*

Make a knot there to secure the yarn. *(photo 3)*

Then insert the needle back through the stuffed piece and out at another point. *(photo 4)*

Finally, cut the yarn. *(photo 5)*

Fasten Off

After the last single crochet stitch is worked, work a slip stitch into the next stitch. Cut the yarn, leaving a tail. With the tail, yarn over and pull the tail through the stitch.

Front and Back Loops

Every stitch has what looks like a 'v' on the top. There are two loops that make up the 'v'. The front loop is the loop closest to you and the back loop is the loop furthest from you. Generally, we work in both loops – under both the front and back loops. Working in either the front or back loops only creates a decorative ridge (made up of the unworked loops).

Note: Work all stitches under both loops unless otherwise instructed.

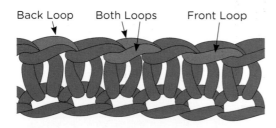

Join With a Slip Knot

Make a slip knot, but do not insert your hook through the loop yet. Insert your hook into the stitch or space indicated and now place the loop of the slip knot on your hook. Gently pull the loop through the stitch, keeping the knot at the back. Continue with the pattern.

Join With a SC (Single Crochet Standing Stitch)

With a slip knot on your hook, insert your hook into the stitch or space specified and pull up a loop (two loops on hook). Yarn over and pull through both loops on your hook (first single crochet made).

Weaving In Yarn Tails

Thread the tail onto a yarn needle. Starting close to where the tail begins, preferably working on the wrong side, weave the tail through the back of several stitches (preferably of the same color) to hide the yarn. When done, trim the tail close to the fabric.

For weaving in ends on an already stuffed piece, you can secure (knot) the yarn close to the piece and then insert the needle through the stuffing and out the other side. If you want, you can do this a few times. When done, cut the yarn close to the toy and let the end disappear inside.

Whipstitch

With both pieces right-side facing, insert your needle through a crocheted stitch on the first piece, from front to back.
Step 1 Bring the needle up through the corresponding stitch on the second piece, from back to front.
Step 2 Insert your needle into the next stitch on the first piece from front to back. Repeat Steps 1 & 2.

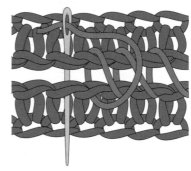

Sew Along (To Make Long Thin Pieces)

In some cases, you will need to make a long, thin, cylindrical piece. In order to achieve this, you crochet a flat piece and sew along the long edges with whipstitches to join them together, creating a cylinder. *(photo 1)*

After crocheting the flat piece as instructed in the pattern, insert the needle into the top right corner and pull the yarn through. *(photo 2)*

2

Insert the needle into the next bottom stitch and through the top one across from it and pull the yarn through. *(photo 3)*

3

Continue working like this until the end of the piece. *(photo 4)*

4

Make a knot to secure the end. *(photo 5)*

5

Magic Ring (Or Adjustable Ring)

Form a loop with the yarn, keeping the tail end of the yarn behind the working yarn (the yarn attached to the ball). *(image 1)*

Insert the hook through the loop (from front to back), and pull the working yarn through the loop (from back to front). Do not tighten up the loop. *(image 2)*

Using the working yarn, make a chain stitch (to secure the ring). This chain stitch does NOT count as the first stitch. *(image 3)*

Work the required stitches into the ring (around both the loop and the tail strand). When all the stitches are done, gently tug the tail end to close the ring, before joining the round (if specified). *(image 4)* Make sure this tail is firmly secured before weaving in the end.

Note: If you prefer, you can use any type of "ring" to start your project (or start with ch-2 and work the first round of stitches into the second chain from the hook). The advantage of using the adjustable Magic Ring is that, when it is tightened, it closes the hole completely.

Tip: Secure your Magic Ring after the first few rounds and before you start stuffing.

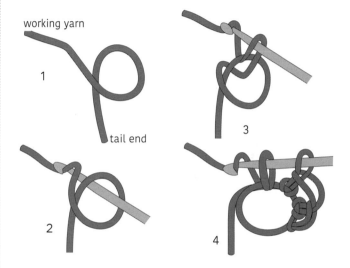

Foundation Chain - Working Around A Chain

One way to crochet an oval piece is by working around both sides of a foundation chain.

Begin by making a foundation chain of the desired length. This chain will form the center of your oval.

Crochet the specified stitches into each chain stitch along the foundation chain. Make sure to follow your pattern instructions for the number and type of stitches to use.

When you reach the end of the chain, you will need to rotate the piece so that you can work into the other side of the chain. Work into the chain loops across the entire length of the other side of the foundation chain.

Once you've completed working around both sides of the foundation chain, continue crocheting in rounds to create an oval piece, following the pattern.

Popcorn Stitch

Make 4 dc into the same stitch or space indicated in the pattern. *(photo 1)*

Once you've completed the 4 stitches, remove your hook from the last stitch worked, leaving the loop. Insert your hook from front to back through the first stitch of the group of stitches you just made. *(photo 2)*

Grab the loop you left behind with your hook. *(photo 3)*

Pull the loop through the first stitch and tighten the loop to create a small bobble or "popcorn". *(photo 4)*

Chain one and continue with your pattern. *(photo 5)*

EMBROIDERY

Straight Stitch

Bring your threaded needle up from the wrong side to the right side of your amigurumi, at the position you want the stitch to start (#1). Insert the needle back into the amigurumi at the position you want the stitch to end (#2). You may go over the same two positions several times to make a thicker straight stitch.

French Knot

Bring your threaded needle up from the wrong side to the right side of the fabric at the position where you want the knot (#1). Wrap the yarn/thread twice around needle. Insert the needle back through the fabric, close to where it came up (almost in the same hole as #1). Gently pull the needle and yarn/thread through the wrapped loops to form the knot.

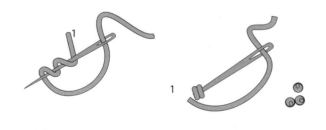

Back Stitch

Bring your threaded needle up from the wrong side to the right side of the fabric (#1). Along the line you want your stitches to be, insert the needle back down a bit behind #1 (#2) and bring it back out a bit ahead of #1 (#3). Insert the needle back down through the original hole (#1) and bring it out a bit ahead again. Repeat all along the desired line you wish to have stitches.

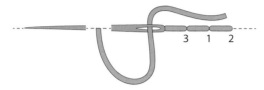

Sewing On Beads as Eyes

As you may notice, I mostly sew on black round beads as eyes for my amigurumi.

Attention: Sewing on beads as eyes is not a child safe method. Embroidering the eyes - like making a couple black stitches in the indicated place - is the only completely child safe method.

You will need two black round beads, a sewing needle and black thread. Thread your sewing needle with the black thread. Tie a knot at the end of the thread. Starting from the back of the amigurumi, bring the needle through to the front at one of the chosen eye positions. Make sure the knot prevents the thread from pulling through. Slide one black bead onto the needle and place it in position. *(photo 1)*

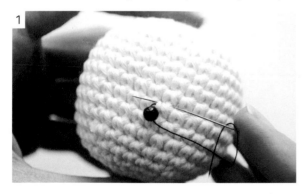

Sew it in place with at least 3-4 stitches to secure the bead in place.

Thread the needle through the amigurumi to the second eye's position. Slide on the second black bead and then sew it in place, just like you did with the first bead. *(photo 2)*

After securing both beads, make a knot and thread the needle to the inside of the amigurumi and carefully pull it through the body. This will hide the remaining thread inside the amigurumi. *(photo 3)*

Note: If you are going to make a smile or a muzzle with the same thread, don't cut it, but pull it through to the spot you want your muzzle/smile to be.

Double check that both beads are securely attached. Gently tug on them to make sure they're properly anchored.

Smile

You will need a sewing needle and black thread. Thread your sewing needle with the black thread or a strand of embroidery floss. Tie a knot at the end of the thread. Starting from the back of the amigurumi, bring the needle through to the front at the chosen position for one side of the smile. Make sure the knot prevents the thread from pulling through. *(photo 1)*

Insert the needle a bit to the right (for the second side of the smile) and thread it back out a bit below and in between the two sides, where you want the bottom of the smile (making sure the loose loop of thread is caught below the needle). *(photo 2)*

Do not tighten the stitch a lot, instead leave it a bit loose. *(photo 3)*

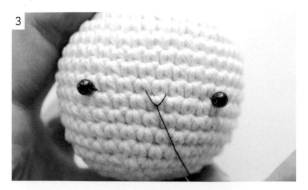

Insert the needle back into the same point it just came out of, making sure to go over the loose loop of thread to secure the smile in place. *(photo 4)*

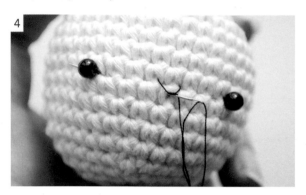

Pull the needle through to where you want to secure the thread and make a tiny knot (I made a knot at the eye, but you can also make it on the side of the smile). *(photo 5)*

Muzzle

Begin by threading a needle and making a diagonal line from point A to point B.

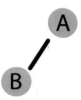

Next, create another diagonal line in the opposite direction, from point C to point B.

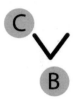

Now, make a horizontal line connecting points C and A at the top of the two diagonal lines.

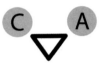

Fill the triangle formed by these lines with 4-5 more horizontal lines to form the nose.

For the mouth, starting at the bottom of the nose (point B in image below), insert the needle a bit to the right (point D), leaving the thread slightly loose. Then, thread the needle back out a bit below and in between points B and D (point E), making sure the loose loop of thread is caught below the needle (just like for a smile).

Insert the needle again at point E, over the loose loop, to anchor this first side of the mouth securely in place.

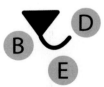

Repeat steps 5 and 6 to the left of the nose, moving from point B to point F and then to point G. Muzzle done!

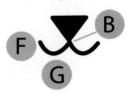

MATERIALS

Hook
All the amigurumi in this book were made with a 2.5 mm hook. You should select a crochet hook size that is suitable for the weight of yarn you have chosen.

Yarn (Tapestry) Needle
A large-eye needle to weave in yarn ends and sew parts of your amigurumi together.

Thread & Needle
For embroidering details and sewing beads.

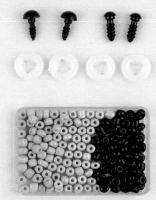

Safety Eyes, Embroidery Floss or Beads
Depending on the design, you can use safety eyes or embroidery floss to create facial features. Another option, that is not baby safe, is beads, that need to be sewn in place.

Scissors
Sharp scissors for cutting yarn and trimming ends.

Yarn
For all the designs in this book I have used HELLO cotton yarn, which is 100% cotton, 25 g / 62.5 m. 50 grams balls are available.

Stuffing
High-quality stuffing material, like polyester fiberfill, to give your amigurumi its shape and volume.

Lake

01. FROG
Finished Size
4.5 cm - 1 ¾"

02. DUCK
Finished Size
4.5 cm - 1 ¾"

03. LAKE
Finished Size
6.5 cm - 2 ½"

04. GREEN PARROT
Finished Size
7 cm - 2 ¾"

05. YELLOW PARROT
Finished Size
5 cm - 2"

06. BUSH
Finished Size
3 cm - 1 ¼"

07. ROCK
Finished Size
1.5 cm - ¾"

08. TREE
Finished Size
9 cm - 3 ½"

09. LOG
Finished Size
9.5 cm - 3 ¾"

10. TREE STUMP
Finished Size
3 cm - 1 ¼"

01. FROG

MATERIALS FOR FROG

» Green yarn (HELLO 169)
» Light cream yarn (HELLO 155)
» 2.5 mm hook
» Two 3 mm black beads & black thread or two 3 mm safety eyes
» Stuffing
» Yarn needle
» Pink embroidery floss & needle

EYES & BODY

With green yarn (HELLO 169)

You start by making the eyes and then join them together and continue to the body.

First Eye

Round 1: Make a magic ring, 6 sc in ring. (6 sc)

Rounds 2-3: *(2 rounds)* Sc in each st around. (6 sc)

Fasten off.

Second Eye + Body

Round 1: Make a magic ring, 6 sc in ring. (6 sc)

Rounds 2-3: *(2 rounds)* Sc in each st around. (6 sc)

Round 4: *(Joining Eyes)* Sc in each of next 3 sts, ch 2, attach with a sc to First Eye, sc in each of next 5 sts of First Eye, sc in each of next 2 ch, sc in each of last 3 sts of Second Eye. (14 sc & 2 ch) *(photos 1-5)*

Round 5: Sc in each of next 3 sts; working on other side of ch-2, sc in each of next 2 ch, sc in each of next 11 sts. (16 sc)

Rounds 6-11: *(6 rounds)* Sc in each st around. (16 sc)

If you are using safety eyes, place them in now at Round 3.

Round 12: [Dec, sc in each of next 2 sts] around. (12 sc)

Stuff.

Round 13: [Dec] around. (6 sc)

Fasten off and sew closed.

ARMS & LEGS (Make 4)

With green yarn (HELLO 169)

Ch 7, sc in 2ⁿᵈ ch from hook, sl st in each of next 5 ch.

Fasten off, leaving a long tail for sewing. *(photo 6)*

BELLY

With light cream yarn (HELLO 155)

Round 1: Make a magic ring, 6 sc in ring; join with sl st to first sc. (6 sc)

Round 2: Ch 1, inc in each st around; join with sl st to first sc. (12 sc)

Fasten off, leaving a long tail for sewing. *(photo 7)*

Quick Assembly Guide

Eyes: Round 3
Smile: Embroider between eyes
Cheeks: Embroider under eyes
Belly: Rounds 8-12
Arms: Rounds 8-9
Legs: Rounds 11-12

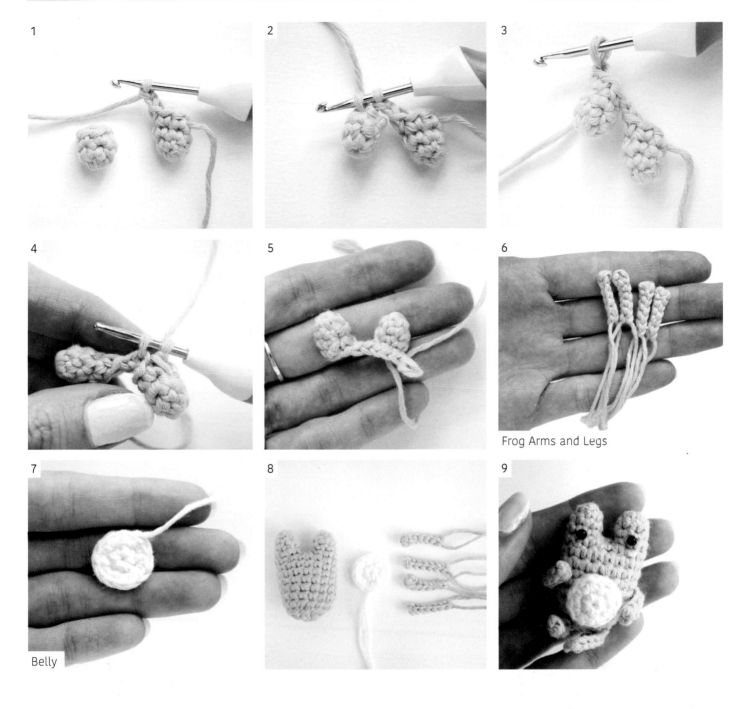

Frog Arms and Legs

Belly

O2. DUCK

MATERIALS FOR DUCK

» Light cream yarn (HELLO 155)
» Dark yellow yarn (HELLO 120)
» 2.5 mm hook
» Two 3 mm black beads & black thread or two 3 mm safety eyes

» Stuffing
» Yarn needle
» Pink embroidery floss & needle

BODY & HEAD

With light cream yarn (HELLO 155)

Round 1: Make a magic ring, 6 sc in ring. (6 sc)

Round 2: Inc in each st around. (12 sc)

Round 3: [Sc in next st, inc in next st] around. (18 sc)

Rounds 4-5: *(2 rounds)* Sc in each st around. (18 sc)

Round 6: *(Neck)* Sc in each of next 8 sts, skip next 10 sts. (8 sc)

Rounds 7-8: *(2 rounds)* Sc in each st around. (8 sc) *(photo 1)*

Round 9: *(Head)* Inc in each st around. (16 sc) *(photo 2)*

Rounds 10-12: *(3 rounds)* Sc in each st around. (16 sc)

If you are using safety eyes, place them in now at Round 10 on the sides of the head, 5 sts apart.

Round 13: [Dec, sc in next st] 4 times, [dec] 2 times. (10 sc)
Stuff.

Round 14: [Dec] around. (5 sc)

Fasten off and sew the head closed.

Stuff the rest of the duck. *(photo 3)*
Using some white yarn, sew the back closed. *(photo 4)*

WINGS (Make 2)

With light cream yarn (HELLO 155)

Ch 4, (sc, hdc) in 3rd ch from hook, (dc, ch 2, sl st) in next ch.

Fasten off, leaving a long tail for sewing. *(photo 5)*

BEAK

With dark yellow yarn (HELLO 120)

Round 1: Ch 4, sc in 2nd ch from hook, sc in each of next 2 ch; working on other side of foundation ch, sc in each of next 3 ch. (6 sc)

Round 2: Sc in each of next 3 sts; end round here. (3 sc)

Fasten off, leaving a long tail for sewing. *(photo 6)*

FEET (Make 2)

With dark yellow yarn (HELLO 120)

Ch 3, sc in 2nd ch from hook, (sc, sl st) in next ch. (2 sc & 1 sl st)

Fasten off, leaving a long tail for sewing.

Quick Assembly Guide

Eyes: Round 10, 5 sts apart
Beak: Rounds 9-10, between eyes
Cheeks: Embroider under eyes
Wings: Rounds 3-4 of body, 5 sts apart
Feet: Rounds 1-2

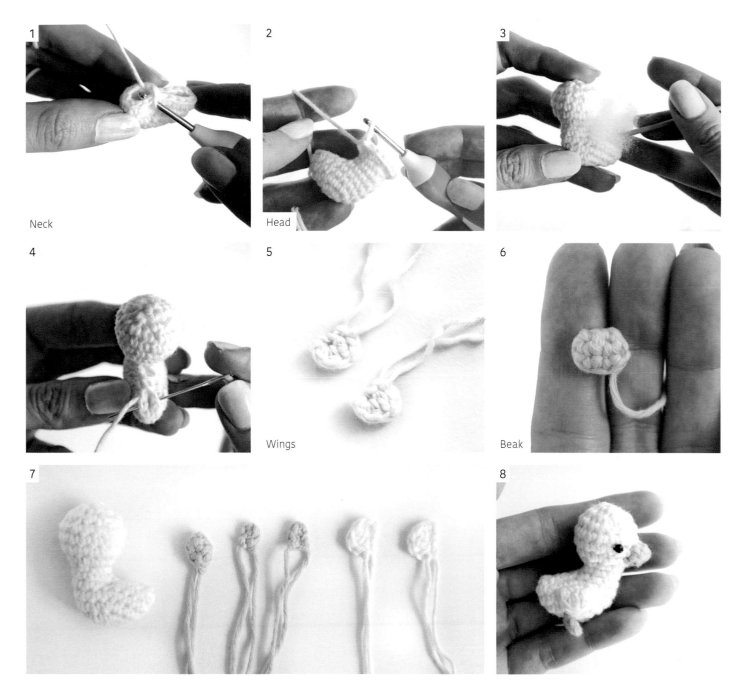

1

Neck

2

Head

3

4

5

Wings

6

Beak

7

8

03. LAKE

MATERIALS FOR LAKE

» Light blue yarn (HELLO 145)
» 2.5 mm hook
» Yarn needle

With light blue yarn (HELLO 145)

Round 1: Make a magic ring, 6 sc in ring. (6 sc)

Round 2: Inc in each st around. (12 sc)

Round 3: [Inc in next st, sc in next st] around. (18 sc)

Round 4: [Inc in next st, sc in each of next 2 sts] around. (24 sc)

Round 5: [Inc in next st, sc in each of next 3 sts] around. (30 sc)

Round 6: [Inc in next st, sc in each of next 4 sts] around. (36 sc)

Round 7: [Inc in next st, sc in each of next 5 sts] around. (42 sc)

Round 8: (2 hdc) in next st, dc in each of next 6 sts, dc-inc in next st, hdc in next st, sc in next st, hdc in next st, dc in each of next 2 sts, dc-inc in next st, dc in each of next 6 sts, dc-inc in next st, dc in each of next 2 sts, hdc in each of next 2 sts, sc in next st, hdc in next st, dc-inc in next st, dc in each of next 6 sts, dc-inc in next st, dc in each of next 2 sts, hdc in each of next 2 sts, sc in each of next 2 sts, sl st in next st. (9 hdc, 34 dc, 4 sc & 1 sl st).

Fasten off and weave in ends.

LAKE ASSEMBLY

04. GREEN PARROT

MATERIALS FOR GREEN PARROT

» Light green yarn (HELLO 129)
» Yellow yarn (HELLO 122)
» Green yarn (HELLO 135)
» Light blue yarn (HELLO 145)
» 2.5 mm hook

» Two 3 mm black beads & black thread or two 3 mm safety eyes
» Stuffing
» Yarn needle
» Pink embroidery floss & needle

BODY

With light green yarn (HELLO 129)

Round 1: Make a magic ring, 6 sc in ring. (6 sc)

Round 2: Inc in each st around. (12 sc)

Round 3: [Sc in next st, inc in next st] around. (18 sc)

Rounds 4-7: *(4 rounds)* Sc in each st around. (18 sc)

Round 8: Sc in each of next 2 sts, dec, sc in each of next 14 sts. (17 sc)

Round 9: Sc in next st, [dec] 2 times, sc each of next 12 sts. (15 sc)

Rounds 10-11: *(2 rounds)* Sc in each st around. (15 sc)

If you are using safety eyes, place them in now at Round 6, 4 sts apart; make sure you place them on the side of the head with the decreases (the curved side).

Round 12: Sc in each of next 2 sts, inc in next st, sc in each of next 12 sts. (16 sc)

Rounds 13-14: *(2 rounds)* Sc in each st around. (16 sc)

Stuff.

Round 15: [Dec, sc in next st] 5 times, sc in last st. (11 sc)

Round 16: [Dec] 5 times, sc in last st. (6 sc)

Fasten off and sew closed.

WINGS (Make 2)

With green yarn (HELLO 135)

Round 1: Make a magic ring, 5 sc in ring. (5 sc)

Round 2: Inc in each st around. (10 sc)

Rounds 3-5: *(3 rounds)* Sc in each st around. (10 sc)

Round 6: [Dec] 2 times, sc in each of next 6 sts. (8 sc)

Round 7: Dec, sc in each of next 6 sts. (7 sc)

Round 8: [Dec] 3 times; end round here. (4 sc)

Fasten off, leaving a long tail for sewing.

BEAK

With yellow yarn (HELLO 122)

Round 1: Make a magic ring, 6 sc in ring. (6 sc)

Round 2: Inc in each of next 2 sts, [dec] 2 times. (6 sc)

Fasten off, leaving a long tail for sewing. Do not stuff.

FEET

With yellow yarn (HELLO 122)

Ch 4, (hdc, sl st) in 3rd ch from hook, (sl st, hdc, ch 2, sl st) in next ch. Fasten off, leaving a long tail for sewing.

TAIL

With light blue yarn (HELLO 145)

Round 1: Ch 3, sc in 2nd ch from hook, inc in next ch; working on other side of foundation ch, sc in next ch, inc in last ch. (6 sc)

Note: *You should now have 3 sc in each of the 2 chains*

Rounds 2-3: *(2 rounds)* Sc in each st around. (6 sc)

Round 4: [Inc in next st, sc in each of next 2 sts] around. (8 sc)

Round 5: [Inc in next st, sc in each of next 3 sts] around. (10 sc)

Round 6: [Inc in next st, sc in each of next 4 sts] around. (12 sc)

Fasten off, leaving a long tail for sewing.

Stuff tail just a bit.

Quick Assembly Guide

Eyes: Round 6, 4 sts apart
Beak: Sew between eyes
Cheeks: Embroider under eyes
Wings: Round 11 of body
Tail: Rounds 15-16 of body

05. YELLOW PARROT

MATERIALS FOR YELLOW PARROT

» Yellow yarn (HELLO 122)
» Dark yellow yarn (HELLO 120)
» Light gray yarn (HELLO 174)
» 2.5 mm hook

» Two 3 mm black beads & black thread or two 3 mm safety eyes
» Stuffing
» Yarn needle
» Pink and white embroidery floss & needle

Special Stitch: Popcorn Stitch - (4 dc) in next st, remove hook, insert hook from front to back into the 1st dc, grab the working loop with hook, pull loop through the dc, ch 1.

BODY

With yellow yarn (HELLO 122)

Round 1: Make a magic ring, 6 sc in ring. (6 sc)

Round 2: Inc in each st around. (12 sc)

Round 3: [Sc in next st, inc in next st] around. (18 sc)

Rounds 4-11: *(8 rounds)* Sc in each st around. (18 sc)

If you are using safety eyes, place them in now at Round 6, 5 sts apart.

Round 12: [Dec, sc in next st] around. (12 sc)

Stuff.

Round 13: [Dec] around. (6 sc)

Fasten off and sew closed.

WINGS (Make 2)

With dark yellow yarn (HELLO 120)

Round 1: Make a magic ring, 5 sc in ring. (5 sc)

Round 2: Inc in each st around. (10 sc)

Rounds 3-5: *(3 rounds)* Sc in each st around. (10 sc)

Round 6: [Dec] 2 times, sc in each of next 6 sts. (8 sc)

Round 7: Dec, sc in each of next 6 sts. (7 sc)

Round 8: [Dec] 3 times; end round here. (4 sc)

Fasten off, leaving a long tail for sewing.

BEAK

With light gray yarn (HELLO 174)

Round 1: Make a magic ring, 3 sc in ring. (3 sc)

Round 2: Inc in each st around. (6 sc)

Round 3: Inc in each of next 2 sts, [dec] 2 times. (6 sc)

Fasten off, leaving a long tail for sewing. Do not stuff.

CREST

With yellow yarn (HELLO 122)

Ch 7, (Popcorn Stitch, sl st) in 3rd ch from hook, sc in next ch, ch 2, (Popcorn Stitch, sl st) in next ch, sc in next ch, ch 2, (Popcorn Stitch, sl st) in next ch.

Fasten off, leaving a long tail for sewing.

FEET

With light gray yarn (HELLO 174)

Ch 4, (hdc, sl st) in 3rd ch from hook,

(sl st, hdc, ch 2, sl st) in next ch.

Fasten off, leaving a long tail for sewing.

TAIL

With yellow yarn (HELLO 122)

[Ch 5, sl st in 2nd ch from hook, sl st in each of next 3 ch] 3 times without breaking yarn; join with sl st to first sl st.

Fasten off, leaving a long tail for sewing.

Quick Assembly Guide

Eyes: Round 6, 5 sts apart

Beak: Sew between eyes, Round 6

Cheeks: Embroider under eyes

Wings: Round 6 of body

Crest: From Round 2 at front of head to Round 4 at back of head

Tail: Round 11 of body

Embroidering Details

Use white embroidery floss or thin yarn to embroider some straight lines on the wings and the belly.

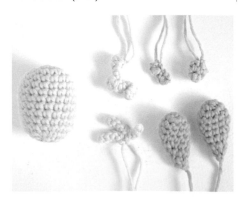

06. BUSH

MATERIALS FOR BUSH

» Green yarn (HELLO 135)
» 2.5 mm hook
» Stuffing
» Yarn needle

With green yarn (HELLO 135)

Round 1: Ch 8, inc in 2nd ch from hook, sc in each of next 6 ch; working on other side of foundation ch, inc in next ch, sc in each of next 6 ch. (16 sc)

Round 2: Sc in next st, inc in next st, sc in each of next 5 sts, inc in next st, sc in next st, inc in next st, sc in each of next 5 sts, inc in next st. (20 sc)

Round 3: Sc in each of next 2 sts, inc in next st, sc in each of next 6 sts, inc in next st, sc in each of next 2 sts, inc in next st, sc in each of next 6 sts, inc in next st. (24 sc)

Round 4: Working in **back loops** only, sc in each st around. (24 sc)

Round 5: Sc in each st around. (24 sc)

Round 6: *(Small Peak)* Sc in each of next 6 sts, ch 5, skip next 14 sts, sc in each of next 4 sts. (10 sc & 1 ch-5) *(photos 1-2)*

Round 7: Sc in each of next 6 sts, sc in each of next 5 ch, sc in each of next 4 sts. (15 sc)

Round 8: [Sc in next st, dec] around. (10 sc)

Round 9: [Dec] around. (5 sc)

Fasten off and sew closed.
Join with a sc in any skipped st from Round 6 *(Starting Large Peak)*; working in both the other side of the ch-5 and the skipped sc sts, continue to sc in each st around. (19 sc) *(photo 3)*

Rounds 7-8: *(2 rounds)* Sc in each st around. (19 sc) *(photo 4)*

Round 9: [Dec, sc in next st] 5 times, [dec] 2 times. (12 sc)

Stuff.

Round 10: [Dec] around. (6 sc)

Fasten off and sew closed.

BUSH ASSEMBLY

1

2

3

4

5

6

07. ROCK

MATERIALS FOR ROCK

» Light gray yarn (HELLO 174)
» 2.5 mm hook
» Stuffing
» Yarn needle

With light gray yarn (HELLO 174)

Round 1: Make a magic ring, 7 sc in ring. (7 sc)

Round 2: Inc in each st around. (14 sc)

Round 3: [Inc in next st, sc in next st] around. (21 sc)

Round 4: [Inc in next st, sc in each of next 2 sts] around. (28 sc)

Rounds 5-6: *(2 rounds)* Sc in each st around. (28 sc)

Round 7: [Sc in each of next 2 sts, dec] around. (21 sc)

Round 8: [Sc in next st, dec] around. (14 sc)

Stuff.

Round 9: [Dec] around. (7 sc)

Fasten off and sew closed.

08. TREE

MATERIALS FOR TREE

» Green yarn (HELLO 171)
» Brown yarn (HELLO 168)
» 2.5 mm hook
» Stuffing
» Yarn needle

With green yarn (HELLO 171)

Round 1: Make a magic ring, 6 sc in ring. (6 sc)

Round 2: Inc in each st around. (12 sc)

Round 3: [Inc in next st, sc in next st] around. (18 sc)

Round 4: [Inc in next st, sc in each of next 2 sts] around. (24 sc)

Round 5: [Inc in next st, sc in each of next 3 sts] around. (30 sc)

Rounds 6-10: *(5 rounds)* Sc in each st around. (30 sc)

Round 11: [Dec, sc in each of next 3 sts] around. (24 sc)

Round 12: [Dec, sc in each of next 2 sts] around. (18 sc)

Round 13: [Inc in next st, sc in each of next 2 sts] around. (24 sc)

Round 14: [Inc in next st, sc in each of next 3 sts] around. (30 sc)

Rounds 15-18: *(4 rounds)* Sc in each st around. (30 sc)

Round 19: [Dec, sc in each of next 3 sts] around. (24 sc)

Round 20: [Dec, sc in each of next 2 sts] around. (18 sc)

Round 21: [Dec, sc in next st] around. (12 sc)

Stuff.

Round 22: Working in **back loops** only, [dec] around. (6 sc)

Fasten off and sew closed. *(photos 1-2)*

Trunk

With brown yarn (HELLO 168)

Round 1: Join with a sc in any of the front loops of Round 21, sc in each of next 3 sts, dec, sc in each of next 4 sts, dec. (10 sc) *(photos 3-6)*

Rounds 2-5: *(4 rounds)* Sc in each st around. (10 sc)

Round 6: [Inc in next st, sc in each of next 3 sts] 2 times, sc in each of last 2 sts. (12 sc)

Round 7: [Inc in next st, sc in each of next 2 sts] around. (16 sc)

Fasten off and weave in ends.

09. LOG

MATERIALS FOR LOG

» Brown yarn (HELLO 168)

» 2.5 mm hook

» Yarn needle

With brown yarn (HELLO 168)

Round 1: Ch 15; join with sl st in first ch to form a ring, sc in each ch around. (15 sc)

Rounds 2-26: *(25 rounds)* Sc in each st around. (15 sc)

Round 27: [Ch 3, sl st in 2nd ch from hook, sc in next ch, skip next st of Round 26, sl st in next st] around.

Fasten off and weave in ends.

» Dark beige yarn (HELLO 158)
» Brown yarn (HELLO 168)
» 2.5 mm hook
» Stuffing
» Yarn needle

With dark beige yarn (HELLO 158)

Round 1: Make a magic ring, 6 sc in ring. (6 sc)

Round 2: Inc in each st around. (12 sc)

Round 3: [Inc in next st, sc in next st] around. (18 sc).

Change to brown yarn (HELLO 168).

Round 4: Working in **back loops** only, sc in each st around. (18 sc)

Rounds 5-6: *(2 rounds)* Sc in each st around. (18 sc)

Round 7: [Sc in each of next 5 sts, inc in next st] around. (21 sc)

Round 8: [Sc in each of next 6 sts, inc in next st] around. (24 sc)

Round 9: [Sc in each of next 7 sts, inc in next st] around. (27 sc)

If your yarn is sturdy enough, you can stop here, fasten off and weave in ends. If your stump needs stuffing to stay in place, continue to Round 10.

Round 10: Working in **back loops** only, [sc in each of next 7 sts, dec] around. (24 sc)

Round 11: [Sc in next st, dec] around. (16 sc)
Stuff.

Round 12: [Dec] around. (8 sc)

Fasten off and sew closed.

Bugs

11. DRAGONFLY
Finished Size
6.5 cm - 2 ½"

12. BEE
Finished Size
6.5 cm - 2 ½"

13. FIREFLY
Finished Size
7 cm - 2 ¾"

14. BUTTERFLY
Finished Size
4.5 cm - 1 ¾"

15. BIG BUTTERFLY
Finished Size
5 cm - 2"

16. ANT
Finished Size
8.5 cm - 3 ¼"

17. LEAF FOR ANT
Finished Size
2 cm - ¾"

18. CATERPILLAR
Finished Size
9.5 cm - 3 ¾"

19. FLOWER
Finished Size
9 cm - 3 ½"

20. BIG FLOWER
Finished Size
12.5 cm - 5"

11. DRAGONFLY

MATERIALS FOR DRAGONFLY

» Light blue yarn (HELLO 145)
» Cream yarn (HELLO 155)
» Lilac yarn (HELLO 141)
» Lime yarn (HELLO 169)
» Pink yarn (HELLO 101)

» 2.5 mm hook
» Two 3 mm black beads & black thread or two 3 mm safety eyes
» Stuffing
» Yarn needle
» Pink embroidery floss & needle

BODY & HEAD

With light blue yarn (HELLO 145)

Round 1: Make a magic ring, 6 sc in ring. (6 sc)

Round 2: Inc in next st, sc in each of next 5 sts. (7 sc)

Rounds 3-10: *(8 rounds)* Sc in each st around. (7 sc)

Round 11: Inc in each st around. (14 sc)

Round 12: [Inc in next st, sc in next st] around. (21 sc)

Rounds 13-16: *(4 rounds)* Sc in each st around. (21 sc)

If you are using safety eyes, place them in now at Round 13, 4 sts apart.

Round 17: [Sc in next st, dec] around. (14 sc)

Stuff.

Round 18: [Dec] around. (7 sc)

Fasten off and sew closed.

WINGS

You start by making each of the 4 wings separately and then join each big wing to a small wing to make two sets of wings.

Big Wing (Make 2)

With cream yarn (HELLO 155)

Round 1: Make a magic ring, 6 sc in ring. (6 sc)

Round 2: [Sc in next st, inc in next st] around. (9 sc)

Round 3: [Sc in each of next 2 sts, inc in next st] around. (12 sc)

Round 4: Sc in each st around. (12 sc)

Round 5: [Sc in each of next 2 sts, dec] around. (9 sc)

Rounds 6-7: *(2 rounds)* Sc in each st around. (9 sc)

Do not stuff. Fasten off.

Small Wing (Make 2)

With cream yarn (HELLO 155)

Round 1: Make a magic ring, 6 sc in ring. (6 sc)

Rounds 2-6: *(5 rounds)* Sc in each st around. (6 sc)

Round 7: *(Joining Wings)* Attach with a sc to Big Wing, dec, [sc in next st, dec] 2 times; working on Small Wing, [sc in next st, dec] 2 times. (10 sc)
(photos 3-4)

Do not stuff. Fasten off, leaving a long tail for sewing.

ANTENNAE

With lilac yarn (HELLO 141)

Cut 4" (10 cm) of lilac yarn and make a knot about ½" (1 cm) from the end.

Thread the other end of the yarn into a needle and insert the yarn into the top of the head at Round 17, above one of the eyes, and pull it through to the other side of Round 17, above the other eye. Make a knot and cut the yarn about ½" (1 cm) away from the knot. *(photos 5-6)*

Quick Assembly Guide

Eyes: Round 13, 4 sts apart
Smile: Embroider between eyes
Cheeks: Embroider under eyes
Antennae: Round 17
Wings: Rounds 17

Embroidering Details

Using lime green, pink and lilac yarn, embroider some horizontal lines on the body of the dragonfly. *(photos 7-9)*

1

2

3

4

Wings

5

Antennae

6

Antennae

7

Embroidery

8

Embroidery

9

Embroidery

10

12. BEE

MATERIALS FOR BEE

» Dark yellow yarn (HELLO 123)
» Brown yarn (HELLO 168)
» Black yarn (HELLO 160)
» Cream yarn (HELLO 155)
» 2.5 mm hook

» Two 3 mm black beads & black thread or two 3 mm safety eyes
» Stuffing
» Yarn needle
» Pink embroidery floss & needle

BODY & HEAD

With dark yellow yarn (HELLO 123)

Round 1: Make a magic ring, 6 sc in ring. (6 sc)

Round 2: Inc in each st around. (12 sc)

Round 3: With brown yarn (HELLO 168), [sc in each of next 5 sts, inc in next st] around. (14 sc)

Round 4: With dark yellow yarn, sc in each st around. (14 sc)

Round 5: With brown yarn, sc in each st around. (14 sc)

Round 6: With dark yellow yarn, sc in each st around. (14 sc)

Round 7: [Sc in next st, dec] 4 times, sc in each of next 2 sts. (10 sc)

Round 8: Inc in each st around. (20 sc)

Round 9: [Sc in each of next 4 sts, inc in next st] around. (24 sc)

Rounds 10-12: *(3 rounds)* Sc in each st around. (24 sc)

Round 13: [Sc in each of next 4 sts, dec] around. (20 sc)

Round 14: [Sc in each of next 2 sts, dec] around. (15 sc)

If you are using safety eyes, place them in now at Round 10, 5 sts apart. Stuff.

Round 15: [Sc in next st, dec] around. (10 sc)
Stuff a bit more.

Round 16: [Dec] around. (5 sc)
Fasten off and sew closed. *(photo 1)*

ARMS (Make 2)

With black yarn (HELLO 160)

Ch 4, sc in 2nd ch from hook, sl st in each of next 2 ch.

Fasten off, leaving a long tail for sewing.

LEGS (Make 2)

With black yarn (HELLO 160)

Ch 3, sl st in 2nd ch from hook, sl st in next ch.

Fasten off, leaving a long tail for sewing.

WINGS (Make 2)

With cream yarn (HELLO 155)

Round 1: Make a magic ring, 6 sc in ring. (6 sc)

Round 2: [Sc in next st, inc in next st] around. (9 sc)

Rounds 3-4: *(2 rounds)* Sc in each st around. (9 sc)

Round 5: [Sc in each of next 2 sts, dec] 2 times, sc in next st. (7 sc)

Round 6: Sc in each st around. (7 sc)

Round 7: Dec, sc in each of next 2 sts, dec, sc in last st. (5 sc)
Do not stuff.
Fasten off, leaving a long tail for sewing. *(photo 2)*

STINGER

With black yarn (HELLO 160)

Make a magic ring, 3 sc in ring; join with sl st to first sc. (3 sc)

Fasten off, leaving a long tail for sewing.

ANTENNAE

With black yarn (HELLO 160)

Cut 4" (10 cm) of black yarn and make a knot about ½" (1 cm) from the end.

Thread the other end of the yarn into a needle and insert the yarn into the top of the head at Round 16, above one of the eyes, and pull it through to the other side of Round 16, above the other eye. Make a knot and cut the yarn about ½" (1 cm) away from the knot. *(photos 4-8)*

Quick Assembly Guide

Eyes: Round 10, 5 sts apart

Smile: Embroider between eyes

Cheeks: Embroider under eyes

Arms: Rounds 5-6

Legs: Round 2

Wings: Rounds 4-6

Antennae: Round 16

Stinger: Round 1

2

Wings

9

Back Wings

10

1

Body

3

4

5

6

7

8

13. FIREFLY

MATERIALS FOR FIREFLY

» Dark yellow yarn (HELLO 123)
» Gray yarn (HELLO 159)
» Cream yarn (HELLO 155)
» 2.5 mm hook
» Two 3 mm black beads & black thread or two 3 mm safety eyes
» Stuffing
» Yarn needle
» Pink embroidery floss & needle

BODY & HEAD

With dark yellow yarn (HELLO 123)

Round 1: Make a magic ring, 6 sc in ring. (6 sc)

Round 2: Inc in each st around. (12 sc)

Rounds 3-5: *(3 rounds)* Sc in each st around. (12 sc)

Round 6: [Sc in next st, dec] around. (8 sc)

Change to gray yarn (HELLO 159)

Round 7: [Sc in next st, inc in next st] around. (12 sc)

Rounds 8-10: *(3 rounds)* Sc in each st around. (12 sc)

Round 11: [Sc in next st, dec] around. (8 sc)

Round 12: Inc in each st around. (16 sc)

Round 13: [Inc in next st, sc in next st] around. (24 sc)

Rounds 14-17: *(4 rounds)* Sc in each st around. (24 sc)

If you are using safety eyes, place them in now at Round 14, 5 sts apart.

Round 18: [Sc in next st, dec] around. (16 sc)

Stuff.

Round 19: [Dec] around. (8 sc)

Fasten off and sew closed.

ARMS (Make 4)

With gray yarn (HELLO 159)

Ch 4, sl st in 2nd ch from hook, sl st in each of next 2 ch.

Fasten off, leaving a long tail for sewing. *(photo 1)*

WINGS

Big Wings (Make 2)

With cream yarn (HELLO 155)

Round 1: Make a magic ring, 6 sc in ring. (6 sc)

Round 2: [Sc in next st, inc in next st] around. (9 sc)

Round 3: [Sc in each of next 2 sts, inc in next st] around. (12 sc)

Round 4: Sc in each st around. (12 sc)

Round 5: [Sc in each of next 2 sts, dec] around. (9 sc)

Rounds 6-7: *(2 rounds)* Sc in each st around. (9 sc)

Round 8: [Sc in next st, dec] around. (6 sc)

Round 9: Sc in each st around. (6 sc)

Do not stuff. Fasten off, leaving a long tail for sewing.

Small Wing (Make 2)

With cream yarn (HELLO 155)

Round 1: Make a magic ring, 6 sc in ring. (6 sc)

Rounds 2-7: *(6 rounds)* Sc in each st around. (6 sc)

Do not stuff. Fasten off, leaving a long tail for sewing.

ANTENNAE

Cut 4" (10 cm) of gray yarn and make a knot about ½" (1 cm) from the end. Thread the other end of the yarn into a needle and insert the yarn into the top of the head at Round 18, above one of the eyes, and pull it through to the other side of Round 18, above the other eye. Make a knot and cut the yarn about ½" (1 cm) away from the knot. *(photo 3)*

Quick Assembly Guide

Eyes: Round 14, 5 sts apart

Smile: Embroider between eyes

Cheeks: Embroider under eyes

Antennae: Round 18

Arms: Rounds 7-8 and Rounds 8-9

Small Wings: Rounds 7-9, 3 sts apart (on the back)

Big Wings: Rounds 9-11, 3 sts apart (on the back)

1

2

3

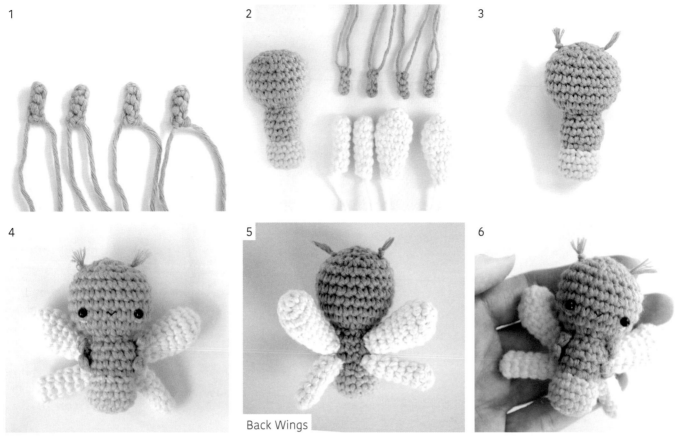

4

5

Back Wings

6

14. BUTTERFLY

MATERIALS FOR BUTTERFLY

» Dark yellow yarn (HELLO 123)
» Pink yarn (HELLO 101)
» 2.5 mm hook
» Two 2 mm black beads & black thread or two 3 mm safety eyes
» Stuffing
» Yarn needle
» Pink and white embroidery floss & needle

BODY & HEAD

With dark yellow yarn (HELLO 123)

Round 1: Make a magic ring, 6 sc in ring. (6 sc)

Rounds 2-5: *(4 rounds)* Sc in each st around. (6 sc)

Round 6: Inc in each st around. (12 sc)

Rounds 7-9: *(3 rounds)* Sc in each st around. (12 sc)

If you are using safety eyes, place them in now at Round 8, 3 sts apart.
Stuff.

Round 10: [Dec] around. (6 sc)

Fasten off and sew closed.

WINGS

You start by making each of the 4 wings separately and then join each big wing to a small wing to make two sets of wings.

Big Wing (Make 2)

With pink yarn (HELLO 101)

Round 1: Make a magic ring, 6 sc in ring. (6 sc)

Round 2: [Sc in next st, inc in next st] around. (9 sc)

Rounds 3-4: *(2 rounds)* Sc in each st around. (9 sc)
Fasten off.

Small Wing (Make 2)

With pink yarn (HELLO 101)

Round 1: Make a magic ring, 6 sc in ring. (6 sc)

Rounds 2-3: *(2 rounds)* Sc in each st around. (6 sc)

Round 4: *(Joining Wings)* Attach with a sc to Big Wing, sc in each of next 2 sts, [dec] 2 times, sc in each of next 2 sts; working on Small Wing, sc in next st, [dec] 2 times, sc in next st. (11 sc)

Round 5: Sc in each of next 3 sts, dec, sc in each of next 6 sts. (10 sc)

Stuff the wings just a bit.

Fasten off, leaving a long tail for sewing.

ANTENNAE

Cut 4" (10 cm) of dark yellow yarn and make a knot about ½" (1 cm) from the end. Thread the other end of the yarn into a needle and insert the yarn into the top of the head at Round 10, above one of the eyes, and pull it through to the other side of Round 10, above the other eye. Make a knot and cut the yarn about ½" (1 cm) away from the knot.

Quick Assembly Guide

Eyes: Round 8, 3 sts apart
Smile: Embroider between eyes
Cheeks: Embroider under eyes
Wings: Rounds 2-5
Antennae: Round 10

Embroidering the Wings

Using white embroidery floss and some simple straight stitches, embroider a few details in each of the butterfly's wings. Remember, each wing is a mirror image of the other, so try to make them look symmetrical.
(photo 3)

 BUTTERFLY ASSEMBLY

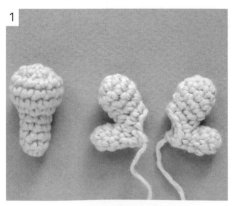
1

2

3

15. BIG BUTTERFLY

MATERIALS FOR BIG BUTTERFLY

» Dark yellow yarn (HELLO 123)
» Light blue yarn (HELLO 145)
» 2.5 mm hook
» Two 3 mm black beads & black thread or two 3 mm safety eyes

» Stuffing
» Yarn needle
» Pink and dark blue embroidery floss & needle

BODY & HEAD

With dark yellow yarn (HELLO 123)

Round 1: Make a magic ring, 6 sc in ring. (6 sc)

Round 2: Inc in each st around. (12 sc)

Round 3: [Inc in next st, sc in next st] around. (18 sc)

Rounds 4-7: *(4 rounds)* Sc in each st around. (18 sc)

Round 8: [Dec, sc in next st] around. (12 sc)

If you are using safety eyes, place them in now at Round 6, 4 sts apart.

Stuff.

Round 9: [Dec] around. (6 sc)

Rounds 10-14: *(5 rounds)* Sc in each st around. (6 sc)

Stuff a bit more.

Fasten off and sew closed.

WINGS

You start by making each of the 4 wings separately and then join each big wing to a small wing to make two sets of wings.

Big Wing (Make 2)

With light blue yarn (HELLO 145)

Round 1: Make a magic ring, 6 sc in ring. (6 sc)

Round 2: [Sc in next st, inc in next st] around. (9 sc)

Rounds 3-4: *(2 rounds)* Sc in each st around. (9 sc)

Fasten off.

Small Wing (Make 2)

With light blue yarn (HELLO 145)

Round 1: Make a magic ring, 6 sc in ring. (6 sc)

Rounds 2-3: *(2 rounds)* Sc in each st around. (6 sc)

Round 4: *(Joining Wings)* Attach with a sc to Big Wing, sc in each of next 2 sts, [dec] 2 times, sc in each of next 2 sts; working on Small Wing, sc in next st, [dec] 2 times, sc in next st. (11 sc)

Round 5: Sc in each of next 3 sts, dec, sc in each of next 6 sts. (10 sc)

Stuff the wings just a bit.

Fasten off, leaving a long tail for sewing.

ANTENNAE

Cut 4" (10 cm) of yellow yarn and make a knot about ½" (1 cm) from the end. Thread the other end of the yarn into a needle and insert the yarn into the top of the head at Round 2, above one of the eyes, and pull it through to the other side of Round 2, above the other eye. Make a knot and cut the yarn about ½" (1 cm) away from the knot. *(photos 2-5)*

Quick Assembly Guide

Eyes: Round 6, 4 sts apart *(photos 6-7)*

Smile: Embroider between eyes, Round 8 *(photos 8-10)*

Cheeks: Embroider under eyes

Wings: Rounds 11-14

Antennae: Round 2

Embroidering the Wings

Using dark blue embroidery floss and some simple straight stitches, embroider a few details in each of the butterfly's wings. Remember, each wing is a mirror image of the other, so try to make them look symmetrical. *(photos 11-12)*

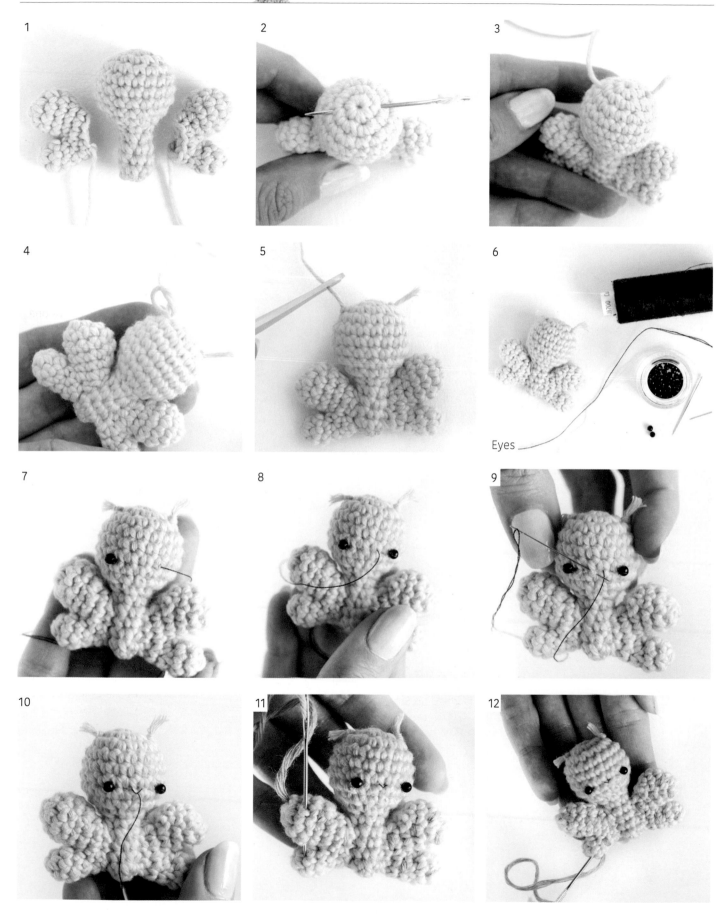

1

2

3

4

5

6

Eyes

7

8

9

10

11

12

16. ANT

MATERIALS FOR ANT

» Brown yarn (HELLO 168)
» 2.5 mm hook
» Two 3 mm black beads & black thread or two 3 mm safety eyes
» Stuffing
» Yarn needle
» Pink embroidery floss & needle

BODY & HEAD

With brown yarn (HELLO 168)

Round 1: Make a magic ring, 6 sc in ring. (6 sc)

Round 2: Inc in each st around. (12 sc)

Round 3: Sc in each of next 5 sts, [inc in next st, sc in next st] 3 times, sc in next st. (15 sc)

Round 4: Sc in each of next 6 sts, [inc in next st, sc in each of next 2 sts] 3 times. (18 sc)

Round 5: Sc in each of next 7 sts, [inc in next st, sc in each of next 3 sts] 2 times, sc in each of next 3 sts. (20 sc)

Round 6: Sc in each st around. (20 sc)

Round 7: (Neck) Sc in each of next 8 sts, skip next 10 sts, sc in each of next 2 sts. (10 sc)

Rounds 8-10: (3 rounds) Sc in each st around. (10 sc)

Round 11: [Dec] 4 times, sc in each of next 2 sts. (6 sc)

Round 12: (Head) Inc in each st around. (12 sc)

Round 13: [Inc in next st, sc in next st] around. (18 sc)

Round 14: [Inc in next st, sc in each of next 2 sts] around. (24 sc)

Rounds 15-18: (4 rounds) Sc in each st around. (24 sc)

If you are using safety eyes, place them in now at Round 15, 5 sts apart.

Round 19: [Sc in each of next 2 sts, dec] around. (18 sc)

Round 20: [Sc in next st, dec] around. (12 sc)

Stuff the head.

Round 21: [Dec] around. (6 sc)
Fasten off and sew the head closed.

Stuff the rest of the ant.

Using some brown yarn, sew the back closed. *(photo 1)*

ANTENNAE

With brown yarn (HELLO 168)

Cut 4" (10 cm) of brown yarn and make a knot about ½" (1 cm) from the end.

Thread the other end of the yarn into a needle and insert the yarn into the top of the head at Round 20, above one of the eyes, and pull it through to the other side of Round 20, above the other eye. Make a knot and cut the yarn about ½" (1 cm) away from the knot.

ARMS & LEGS (Make 6)

With brown yarn (HELLO 168)

Row 1: Ch 4, sc in 2nd ch from hook, sc in each of next 2 ch. (3 sc)

Row 2: Ch 1, turn, sc in each of next 3 sts. (3 sc)

Fasten off, leaving a long tail for sewing.

Sew along the long edges (whipstitch) to form a long cylinder. *(photos 3-5)*

Quick Assembly Guide

Eyes: Round 15, 5 sts apart
Smile: Embroider between eyes
Cheeks: Embroider under eyes
Antennae: Round 20
Arms: Rounds 6-7
Legs: Rounds 1-2

1

Sew

2

Body

3

Legs

4

5

6

7

8

Ant Leaf

9

17. LEAF FOR ANT

MATERIALS FOR LEAF FOR ANT

» Green yarn (HELLO 135)

» 2.5 mm hook

» Yarn needle

With green yarn (HELLO 135)

Ch 5, sl st in 2nd ch from hook, hdc in next ch, sc in next ch, sl st in last ch, ch 1; working on other side of foundation ch, sl st in next ch, sc in next ch, hdc in next ch, sl st in last ch, ch 3, sl st in 2nd ch from hook, sl st in next ch.

Fasten off and weave in ends.

18. CATERPILLAR

MATERIALS FOR CATERPILLAR

- » Lime yarn (HELLO 169)
- » 2.5 mm hook
- » Two 3 mm black beads & black thread or two 3 mm safety eyes
- » Stuffing
- » Yarn needle
- » Pink embroidery floss & needle

BODY & HEAD

With lime yarn (HELLO 169)

Round 1: Make a magic ring, 6 sc in ring. (6 sc)

Round 2: Inc in each st around. (12 sc)

Round 3: [Inc in next st, sc in next st] around. (18 sc)

Round 4: [Inc in next st, sc in each of next 2 sts] around. (24 sc)

Rounds 5-9: (5 rounds) Sc in each st around. (24 sc)

Round 10: [Sc in each of next 2 sts, dec] around. (18 sc)

If you are using safety eyes, place them in now at Round 7, after the 1st and 20th sts of the round (5 sts apart).

Round 11: [Sc in next st, dec] around. (12 sc)

Stuff.

Round 12: [Dec] around. (6 sc)

Round 13: Inc in each st around. (12 sc)

Round 14: [Sc in next st, inc in next st] around. (18 sc)

Round 15: Sc in each of next 4 sts, inc in next st, sc in each of next 7 sts, dec, sc in each of next 4 sts. (18 sc)

Rounds 16-17: (2 rounds) Sc in each st around. (18 sc)

Round 18: [Sc in next st, dec] around. (12 sc)

Stuff.

Round 19: [Dec] around. (6 sc)

Round 20: Inc in each st around. (12 sc)

Round 21: [Sc in next st, inc in next st] around. (18 sc)

Round 22: Sc in each of next 4 sts, inc in next st, sc in each of next 7 sts, dec,

sc in each of next 4 sts. (18 sc)

Rounds 23-24: (2 rounds) Sc in each st around. (18 sc)

Round 25: [Sc in next st, dec] around. (12 sc)

Stuff.

Round 26: [Dec] around. (6 sc)

Fasten off and sew closed.

ARMS & LEGS (Make 6)

With lime yarn (HELLO 169)

Round 1: Make a magic ring, 5 sc in ring. (5 sc)

Rounds 2-3: (2 rounds) Sc in each st around. (5 sc)

Do not stuff.

Fasten off, leaving a long tail for sewing.

ANTENNAE

With lime yarn (HELLO 169)

Cut 4" (10 cm) of lime yarn and make a knot about ½" (1 cm) from the end.

Thread the other end of the yarn into a needle and insert the yarn into the top of the head at Round 2, above one of the eyes, and pull it through to the other side of Round 2, above the other eye. Make a knot and cut the yarn about ½" (1 cm) away from the knot.

Quick Assembly Guide

Eyes: Round 7, 5 sts apart

Smile: Embroider between eyes

Cheeks: Embroider under eyes

Antennae: Round 2

1st set of legs: Rounds 13-15, 2 sts apart

2nd set of legs: Rounds 20-22, 2 sts apart

3rd set of legs: Rounds 25-26, 1 st apart

Caterpillar Leaf

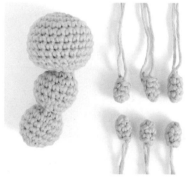

19. FLOWER

MATERIALS FOR FLOWER

- » Blue yarn (HELLO 148)
- » Green yarn (HELLO 135)
- » Dark yellow yarn (HELLO 123)
- » 2.5 mm hook
- » Yarn needle

With blue yarn (HELLO 148)

Round 1: Make a magic ring, 6 sc in ring. (6 sc)

Round 2: Inc in each st around. (12 sc)

Round 3: [Sc in next st, inc in next st] around. (18 sc)

Round 4: [Sc in each of next 2 sts, inc in next st] around. (24 sc)

Rounds 5-9: *(5 rounds)* Sc in each st around. (24 sc)

Round 10: [Sl st in next st, skip next st, (5 hdc) in next st, skip next st] around. (6 sl st & 30 hdc)

Fasten off and weave in ends.

STAMENS (Make 2)

With dark yellow yarn (HELLO 123)

Ch 11, inc in 2nd ch from hook, sl st in each of next 9 ch.

Fasten off, leaving a long tail for sewing.

Sew both stamens inside the flower at the base, 1 st apart. *(photo 1)*

STEM

With green yarn (HELLO 135)

Row 1: Ch 15, sc in 2nd ch from hook, sc in each of next 13 ch. (14 sc)

Row 2: Ch 1, turn, sc in each of next 14 sts. (14 sc)

Fasten off, leaving a long tail for sewing.

Sew along the long edges (whipstitch) to form a long cylinder.

Sew to the bottom of the flower, at Round 1.

LEAF

With green yarn (HELLO 135)

Ch 5, sl st in 2nd ch from hook, hdc in next ch, sc in next ch, sl st in last ch, ch 1; working on other side of foundation ch, sl st in next ch, sc in next ch, hdc in next ch, sl st in last ch.

Fasten off, leaving a long tail for sewing. *(photo 2)*

Sew on the stem. *(photo 4)*

1

2

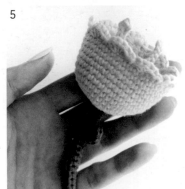

Leaf

3

4

5

6

20. BIG FLOWER

MATERIALS FOR BIG FLOWER

» Pink yarn (HELLO 101)
» Green yarn (HELLO 135)
» Dark yellow yarn (HELLO 123)
» 2.5 mm hook
» Yarn needle

With pink yarn (HELLO 101)

Round 1: Make a magic ring, 6 sc in ring. (6 sc)

Round 2: Inc in each st around. (12 sc)

Round 3: [Sc in next st, inc in next st] around. (18 sc)

Round 4: [Sc in each of next 2 sts, inc in next st] around. (24 sc)

Round 5: [Sc in each of next 3 sts, inc in next st] around. (30 sc)

Round 6: [Sc in each of next 4 sts, inc in next st] around. (36 sc)

Rounds 7-13: *(7 rounds)* Sc in each st around. (36 sc)

Round 14: [Sl st in next st, skip next st, (5 hdc) in next st, skip next st] around. (9 sl st & 45 hdc)

Fasten off and weave in ends.

STAMENS (MAKE 2)

With dark yellow yarn (HELLO 123)

Ch 16, inc in 2nd ch from hook, sl st in each of next 14 ch.

Fasten off, leaving a long tail for sewing. Sew both stamens inside the flower at the base, 1 st apart.

STEM

With green yarn (HELLO 135)

Row 1: Ch 23, sc in 2nd ch from hook, sc in each of next 21 ch. (22 sc)

Row 2: Ch 1, turn, sc in each of next 22 sts. (22 sc)

Fasten off, leaving a long tail for sewing. Sew along the long edges (whipstitch) to form a long cylinder.

Sew to the bottom of the flower, at Round 1.

LEAF

With green yarn (HELLO 135)

Ch 5, sl st in 2nd ch from hook, hdc in next ch, sc in next ch, sl st in last ch, ch 1; working on other side of foundation ch, sl st in next ch, sc in next ch, hdc in next ch, sl st in last ch.

Fasten off, leaving a long tail for sewing.

Sew the leaf on the stem.

Birthday

21. BEAR
Finished Size
8.5 cm - 3 ¼"

22. BUNNY
Finished Size
7 cm - 2 ¾"

23. FOX
Finished Size
7cm - 2 ¾"

24. MEERKAT
Finished Size
9.5 cm - 3 ¾"

25. SQUIRREL
Finished Size
7 cm - 2 ¾"

26. CAKE
Finished Size
5 cm - 2"

27. GIFT 1
Finished Size
2.5 cm - 1"

28. GIFT 2
Finished Size
2 cm - ¾"

29. GARLAND
Finished Size
23 cm - 9"

30. PARTY HATS
Finished Size
1.5 cm - ¾"

21. BEAR

MATERIALS FOR BEAR

» Brown yarn (HELLO 168)
» Cream yarn (HELLO 155)
» 2.5 mm hook
» Two 4 mm black beads & black thread or two 4 mm safety eyes
» Stuffing
» Yarn needle
» Pink embroidery floss & needle

BODY & LEGS

With brown yarn (HELLO 168)

Round 1: Ch 6, sc in 2nd ch from hook, sc in each of next 3 ch, inc in last ch; working on other side of foundation ch, sc in each of next 4 ch, inc in last ch. (12 sc)

Round 2: [Inc in next st, sc in each of next 3 sts, inc in next st, sc in next st] 2 times. (16 sc)

Round 3: Sc in next st, inc in next st, sc in each of next 4 sts, inc in next st, sc in each of next 2 sts, inc in next st, sc in each of next 4 sts, inc in next st, sc in next st. (20 sc)

Round 4: Sc in each of next 2 sts, inc in next st, sc in each of next 5 sts, inc in next st, sc in each of next 3 sts, inc in next st, sc in each of next 5 sts, inc in next st, sc in next st. (24 sc)

Rounds 5-15: *(11 rounds)* Sc in each st around. (24 sc)

If you are using safety eyes, place them in now at Round 7, 7 sts apart.

Round 16: *(First Leg)* Sc in each of next 5 sts, skip next 16 sts, sc in each of next 3 sts. (8 sc)

Rounds 17-20: *(4 rounds)* Sc in each st around. (8 sc)

Fasten off and sew the leg closed using only the **back loops**.

Stuff.

Second Leg

You will now return to the sts you skipped during Round 16 of the body to make the Second Leg.

Note: Between the legs there will be a gap 4 sc wide (4 sc on each side) that will be sewn closed later.

Round 16: *(Second Leg)* Skip next 4 sts after First Leg; join with a sc *(now beginning of round; photo 1)*, sc in each of next 7 sts, skip last 4 sts. (8 sc)

Rounds 17-20: *(4 rounds)* Sc in each st around. (8 sc)

Stuff.
Fasten off and sew the leg closed using only the **back loops**.

Sew the gap between the legs closed.

ARMS (Make 2)

With brown yarn (HELLO 168)

Round 1: Make a magic ring, 7 sc in ring. (7 sc)

Rounds 2-6: *(5 rounds)* Sc in each st around. (7 sc)

Do not stuff.

Fasten off, leaving a long tail for sewing.

EARS (Make 2)

With brown yarn (HELLO 168)

Round 1: Make a magic ring, 6 sc in ring. (6 sc)

Round 2: Sc in each of next 3 sts, inc in next st, sc in each of last 2 sts. (7 sc)

Round 3: Sc in each of next 5 sts, dec. (6 sc)

Do not stuff.

Fasten off, leaving a long tail for sewing.

BELLY

With cream yarn (HELLO 155)

Ch 6, dc-inc in 4th ch from hook, dc in next ch, (3 dc) in last ch; working on other side of foundation ch, dc-inc in next ch, dc in next ch, (3 dc) in last ch; join with sl st to first st. (12 dc)
Fasten off, leaving a long tail for sewing.

MUZZLE

With cream yarn (HELLO 155)

Round 1: Make a magic ring, 5 sc in ring. (5 sc)

Round 2: Inc in each of next 2 sts, sc in each of next 3 sts. (7 sc)

Round 3: Sc in each of next 2 sts, inc in each of next 2 sts, sc in each of next 3 sts. (9 sc)

Stuff just a bit.

Fasten off, leaving a long tail for sewing.

Quick Assembly Guide

Eyes: Round 7, 7 sts apart

Cheeks: Embroider under eyes

Muzzle: Rounds 6-10

Ears: Rounds 1-3, 5 sts apart

Belly: Rounds 12-16

Arms: Rounds 9-12

Embroidering Details

You can embroider details on your bear by splitting your yarn (use 3 stands) or use embroidery floss.

Using simple straight stitches, make 3 claws in each leg and hair on top of the head. *(photos 3-5)*

Embroidering Muzzle

Basic sewing thread is the best for embroidering muzzles on small amigurumi. It makes them look neater than using a thick yarn, or even embroidery floss. It requires more work to fill in the nose, but it is worth it (see page 16). *(photos 6-7)*

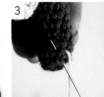

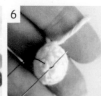
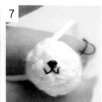

22. BUNNY

MATERIALS FOR BUNNY

» Gray yarn (HELLO 174)
» Cream yarn (HELLO 155)
» 2.5 mm hook
» Two 2 mm black beads & black thread or two 3 mm safety eyes

» Stuffing
» Yarn needle
» Pink embroidery floss & needle
» Dark gray and white yarn (you can split to make thinner) or embroidery floss

LEGS & BODY

With gray yarn (HELLO 174)

You start by making the legs and then join them together and continue to the body.

First Leg

Round 1: Make a magic ring, 6 sc in ring. (6 sc)

Rounds 2-3: *(2 rounds)* Sc in each st around. (6 sc)

Fasten off.

Second Leg + Body

Round 1: Make a magic ring, 6 sc in ring. (6 sc)

Rounds 2-3: *(2 rounds)* Sc in each st around. (6 sc)

Round 4: *(Joining Legs)* Sc in each of next 2 sts, attach with a sc to First Leg, sc in each of next 5 sts, sc in each of last 4 sts of Second Leg. (12 sc)

Rounds 5-8: *(4 rounds)* Sc in each st around. (12 sc)
Stuff.

Round 9: [Dec, sc in next st] around. (8 sc)
Stuff a bit more.

Fasten off, leaving a long tail for sewing.

ARMS (Make 2)

With gray yarn (HELLO 174)

Round 1: Make a magic ring, 5 sc in ring. (5 sc)

Rounds 2-3: *(2 rounds)* Sc in each st around. (5 sc)

Fasten off, leaving a long tail for sewing.

BELLY

With cream yarn (HELLO 155)

Round 1: Make a magic ring, 5 sc in ring. (5 sc)

Round 2: Inc in each st around. (10 sc)

Fasten off, leaving a long tail for sewing.

HEAD

With gray yarn (HELLO 174)

Round 1: Make a magic ring, 6 sc in ring. (6 sc)

Round 2: Inc in each st around. (12 sc)

Round 3: [Sc in next st, inc in next st] around. (18 sc)

Rounds 4-7: *(4 rounds)* Sc in each st around. (18 sc)

If you are using safety eyes, place them in now at Round 6, 3 sts apart.

Round 8: [Dec, sc in next st] around. (12 sc)
Stuff.

Round 9: [Dec] around. (6 sc)

Fasten off and sew closed. Sew the head to the body.

EARS (Make 2)

With gray yarn (HELLO 174)

Round 1: Make a magic ring, 4 sc in ring. (4 sc)

Round 2: Inc in each st around. (8 sc)

Round 3: Sc in each st around. (8 sc)

Round 4: [Sc in each of next 2 sts, dec] around. (6 sc)

Round 5: Sc in each st around. (6 sc)
Do not stuff.

Fasten off, leaving a long tail for sewing.

Quick Assembly Guide

Eyes: Round 6 of head, 3 sts apart

Nose: Embroider between eyes, Round 5 of head

Cheeks: Embroider under eyes

Belly: Rounds 3-7 of body

Arms: Rounds 7-8 of body

Embroidering Details

You can embroider details on your bunny by splitting your yarn (use 3 strands) or use embroidery floss. Using simple straight stitches, make some random white and dark gray stitches on the head to look like hair.

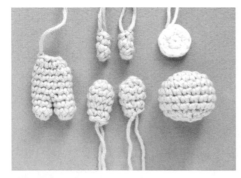

23. FOX

MATERIALS FOR FOX

» Cinnamon yarn (HELLO 166)
» White yarn (HELLO 154)
» 2.5 mm hook
» Two 2 mm black beads & black thread or two 3 mm safety eyes
» Stuffing
» Yarn needle
» Pink embroidery floss & needle

LEGS & BODY

With cinnamon yarn (HELLO 166)

You start by making the legs and then join them together and continue to the body.

First Leg

Round 1: Make a magic ring, 6 sc in ring. (6 sc)

Rounds 2-3: *(2 rounds)* Sc in each st around. (6 sc)

Fasten off.

Second Leg + Body

Round 1: Make a magic ring, 6 sc in ring. (6 sc)

Rounds 2-3: *(2 rounds)* Sc in each st around. (6 sc)

Round 4: *(Joining Legs)* Sc in each of next 2 sts, attach with a sc to First Leg, sc in each of next 5 sts, sc in each of last 4 sts of Second Leg. (12 sc) *(photos 1-2)*

Rounds 5-8: *(4 rounds)* Sc in each st around. (12 sc)

Stuff.

Round 9: [Dec, sc in next st] around. (8 sc)

Stuff a bit more.

Fasten off, leaving a long tail for sewing.

ARMS (Make 2)

With cinnamon yarn (HELLO 166)

Round 1: Make a magic ring, 5 sc in ring. (5 sc)

Rounds 2-3: *(2 rounds)* Sc in each st around. (5 sc)

Fasten off, leaving a long tail for sewing.

HEAD

With cinnamon yarn (HELLO 166)

Round 1: Make a magic ring, 6 sc in ring. (6 sc)

Round 2: Inc in each st around. (12 sc)

Round 3: [Sc in next st, inc in next st] around. (18 sc)

Rounds 4-5 *(2 rounds)* Sc in each st around. (18 sc)

Round 6: With white yarn (HELLO 154), sc in each of next 3 sts; with cinnamon yarn, sc in next st; with white yarn, sc in each of next 3 sts; with cinnamon yarn, sc in each of next 11 sts. (18 sc)

Round 7: With white yarn, sc in each of next 8 sts; with cinnamon yarn, sc in each of next 10 sts. (18 sc)

If you are using safety eyes, place them in now at Round 6, after the 1st white st of the round and before the last white st (3 sts apart).

Round 8: With white yarn, [dec, sc in next st] 2 times, dec; with cinnamon yarn, sc in next st, [dec, sc in next st] 3 times. (12 sc)

Stuff.

Round 9: [Dec] around. (6 sc)

Fasten off and sew closed. *(photo 4)* Sew the head to the body.

TAIL

With white yarn (HELLO 154)

Round 1: Make a magic ring, 4 sc in ring. (4 sc)

Round 2: [Inc in next st, sc in next st] around. (6 sc).
Change to cinnamon yarn.

Round 3: Sc in each st around. (6 sc)

Round 4: [Sc in next st, dec] around. (4 sc)

Fasten off, leaving a long tail for sewing.

EARS (Make 2)

With cinnamon yarn (HELLO 166)

Round 1: Make a magic ring, 4 sc in ring. (4 sc)

Round 2: Inc in next st, sc in each of next 3 sts. (5 sc)

Round 3: [Inc in next st, sc in next st] 2 times, inc in last st. (8 sc)

Do not stuff.

Fasten off, leaving a long tail for sewing.

SNOUT

With cinnamon yarn (HELLO 166)

Round 1: Make a magic ring, 4 sc in ring; with white yarn, 3 sc in ring. (7 sc)

Fasten off, leaving a long tail for sewing.

With black thread and a sewing needle, embroider the nose on the end of the snout. Form the snout with your fingers to have a more conical shape and sew it in place.

Quick Assembly Guide

Eyes: Round 6 of head, 3 sts apart

Snout: Rounds 5-7 of head, 1 st away from each eye

Nose: Embroider on snout

Cheeks: Embroider under eyes

Arms: Rounds 7-8 of body

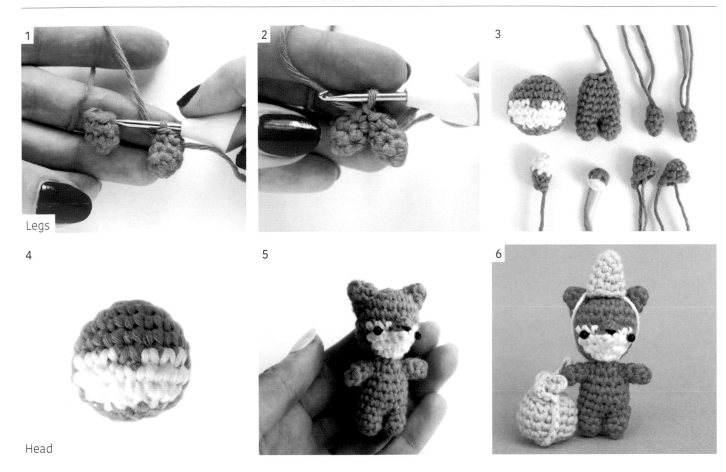

1

2

3

Legs

4

5

6

Head

24. MEERKAT

MATERIALS FOR MEERKAT

» Beige yarn (HELLO 165)
» 2.5 mm hook
» Two 3 mm black beads & black thread or two 3 mm safety eyes

» Stuffing
» Yarn needle
» Pink and black embroidery floss & needle

BODY

With beige yarn (HELLO 165)

Round 1: Make a magic ring, 6 sc in ring. (6 sc)

Round 2: Inc in each st around. (12 sc)

Round 3: [Inc in next st, sc in next st] around. (18 sc)

Round 4: Sc in each of next 8 sts, inc in each of next 2 sts, sc in each of next 8 sts. (20 sc)

Round 5: Sc in each st around. (20 sc)

Round 6: Sc in each of next 9 sts, dec, sc in each of next 9 sts. (19 sc)

Round 7: Sc in each of next 7 sts, dec, sc in next st, dec, sc in each of next 7 sts. (17 sc)

Round 8: Sc in each of next 6 sts, dec, sc in next st, dec, sc in each of next 6 sts. (15 sc)

Round 9: Sc in each of next 5 sts, dec, sc in next st, dec, sc in each of next 5 sts. (13 sc)

If you are using safety eyes, place them in now at Round 5, after the 6th and 12th sts of the round (5 sts apart); make sure you place them on the side of the head with the increases and decreases (the curved side).

Round 10: Sc in each of next 5 sts, dec, sc in each of next 6 sts. (12 sc)

Rounds 11-19: (9 rounds) Sc in each st around. (12 sc)

Stuff.

Round 20: (First Leg) Sc in each of next 3 sts, skip next 6 sts, sc in each of next 3 sts. (6 sc)

Rounds 21-23: (3 rounds) Sc in each st around. (6 sc)
Fasten off and sew closed.

Second Leg

You will now return to the sts you skipped during Round 20 of the body to make the Second Leg.

Round 20: (Second Leg) Join with a sc in any skipped st (now beginning of round; photo 2), sc in each of next 5 sts. (6 sc)

Rounds 21-23: (3 rounds) Sc in each st around. (6 sc)

Fasten off and sew closed.

ARMS (Make 2)

With beige yarn (HELLO 165)

Row 1: Ch 8, sc in 2nd ch from hook, sc in each of next 6 ch. (7 sc)

Row 2: Ch 1, turn, sc in each of next 7 sts. (7 sc)

Fasten off, leaving a long tail for sewing.

Sew along the long edges (whipstitch) to form a long cylinder. (photos 3-5)

TAIL

With beige yarn (HELLO 165)

Round 1: Make a magic ring, 4 sc in ring. (4 sc)

Round 2: Inc in next st, sc in each of next 3 sts. (5 sc)

Round 3: Inc in next st, sc in each of next 4 sts. (6 sc)

Round 4: Inc in next st, sc in each of next 5 sts. (7 sc)

Round 5: Inc in next st, sc in each of next 6 sts. (8 sc)

Round 6: Inc in next st, sc in each of next 7 sts. (9 sc)

Round 7: Inc in next st, sc in each of next 8 sts. (10 sc)

Round 8: Inc in next st, sc in each of next 9 sts. (11 sc)

Round 9: Inc in next st, sc in each of next 10 sts. (12 sc)

Fasten off, leaving a long tail for sewing.
Stuff.

EARS (Make 2)

With beige yarn (HELLO 165)

Round 1: Make a magic ring, 3 sc in ring. (3 sc)

Fasten off, leaving a long tail for sewing.

Quick Assembly Guide

Eyes: Round 5, 5 sts apart

Cheeks: Embroider under eyes

Nose: Embroider between eyes

Ears: Rounds 4-5, on the sides

Arms: Rounds 13-14

Tail: Rounds 15-19

Embroidering Details

Using some black embroidery floss, embroider a nose with horizontal straight stitches, one under the other, about 3 stitches long. Next, embroider 2 curved lines under the nose to complete the muzzle. Finally, using some white thread, make a couple of straight stitches over the nose.

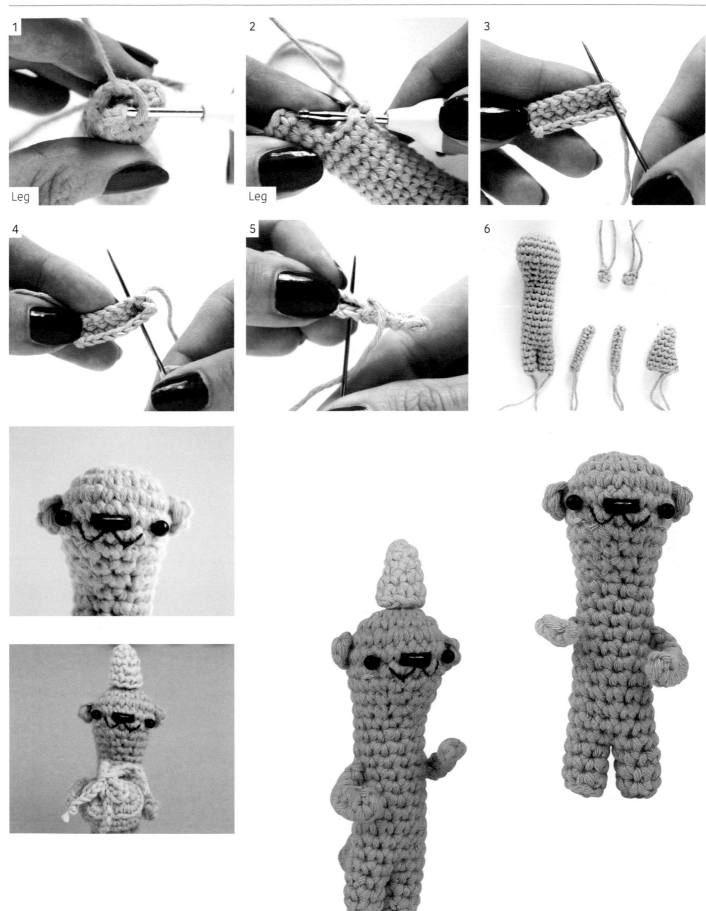

1

Leg

2

Leg

3

4

5

6

25. SQUIRREL

MATERIALS FOR SQUIRREL

» Light brown yarn (HELLO 167)
» 2.5 mm hook
» Two 2 mm black beads & black thread or two 3 mm safety eyes

» Stuffing
» Yarn needle
» Pink embroidery floss & needle

LEGS & BODY

With light brown yarn (HELLO 167)

You start by making the legs and then join them together and continue to the body.

First Leg

Round 1: Make a magic ring, 6 sc in ring. (6 sc)

Rounds 2-3: *(2 rounds)* Sc in each st around. (6 sc)

Fasten off.

Second Leg + Body

Round 1: Make a magic ring, 6 sc in ring. (6 sc)

Rounds 2-3: *(2 rounds)* Sc in each st around. (6 sc)

Round 4: *(Joining Legs)* Sc in each of next 2 sts, attach with a sc to First Leg, sc in each of next 5 sts, sc in each of last 4 sts of Second Leg. (12 sc)

Rounds 5-8: *(4 rounds)* Sc in each st around. (12 sc)

Stuff.

Round 9: [Dec, sc in next st] around. (8 sc)

Stuff a bit more.

Fasten off, leaving a long tail for sewing.

ARMS (Make 2)

With light brown yarn (HELLO 167)

Round 1: Make a magic ring, 5 sc in ring. (5 sc)

Rounds 2-3: *(2 rounds)* Sc in each st around. (5 sc)

Fasten off, leaving a long tail for sewing.

HEAD

With light brown yarn (HELLO 167)

Round 1: Make a magic ring, 6 sc in ring. (6 sc)

Round 2: Inc in each st around. (12 sc)

Round 3: [Sc in next st, inc in next st] around. (18 sc)

Rounds 4-5: *(2 rounds)* Sc in each st around. (18 sc)

Round 6: [Sc in next st, inc in next st] 2 times, sc in each of next 14 sts. (20 sc)

Round 7: [Sc in each of next 2 sts, inc in next st] 2 times, sc in each of next 14 sts. (22 sc)

If you are using safety eyes, place them in now at Round 6, one before the 1st inc and the other after the 2nd inc of the round (4 sts apart).

Round 8: [Dec, sc in next st] 7 times, sc in last st. (15 sc)

Stuff.

Round 9: [Dec] 7 times, sc in last st. (8 sc)

Fasten off and sew closed. Sew the head to the body.

EARS (Make 2)

With light brown yarn (HELLO 167)

Round 1: Make a magic ring, 4 sc in ring. (4 sc)

Round 2: Inc in next st, sc in each of next 3 sts. (5 sc)

Round 3: [Inc in next st, sc in next st] 2 times, inc in last st. (8 sc)

Do not stuff.

Fasten off, leaving a long tail for sewing.

TAIL

With light brown yarn (HELLO 167)

Round 1: Make a magic ring, 4 sc in ring. (4 sc)

Round 2: [Sc in next st, inc in next st] around. (6 sc)

Round 3: [Sc in next st, inc in next st] around. (9 sc)

Round 4: [Sc in each of next 2 sts, inc in next st] around. (12 sc)

Rounds 5-6: *(2 rounds)* Sc in each st around. (12 sc)

Round 7: Inc in each of next 2 sts, sc in each of next 3 sts, [dec] 2 times, sc in each of next 3 sts. (12 sc)

Round 8: Sc in each of next 7 sts, dec, sc in each of next 3 sts. (11 sc)

Round 9: Sc in each of next 6 sts, [dec] 2 times, sc in last st. (9 sc)

Round 10: Sc in next st, [dec] 2 times, sc in each of next 4 sts. (7 sc)

Round 11: Sc in next st, dec, sc in each of next 2 sts, inc in next st, sc in last st. (7 sc)

Round 12: Dec, sc in each of next 5 sts. (6 sc)
Round 13: Dec, sc in each of next 4 sts. (5 sc)
Do not stuff.

Fasten off, leaving a long tail for sewing.

Quick Assembly Guide

Eyes: Round 6 of head, 4 sts apart
Nose: Embroider between eyes
Cheeks: Embroider under eyes
Arms: Rounds 7-8 of body

Tail: Rounds 5-6 of body
Ears: Rounds 1-4 of head

SQUIRREL ASSEMBLY

26. CAKE

MATERIALS FOR CAKE

» Cream yarn (HELLO 156)
» Pink yarn (HELLO 109)
» Blue yarn (HELLO 145)
» Gold yarn (HELLO 123)

» 2.5 mm hook
» Stuffing
» Yarn needle

CAKE

With cream yarn (HELLO 156)

Round 1: Make a magic ring, 6 sc in ring. (6 sc)

Round 2: Inc in each st around. (12 sc)

Round 3: [Inc in next st, sc in next st] around. (18 sc)

Round 4: [Inc in next st, sc in each of next 2 sts] around. (24 sc)

Round 5: Working in **back loops** only, sc in each st around. (24 sc)

Rounds 6-11: *(6 rounds)* Sc in each st around. (24 sc)

Round 12: Working in **back loops** only, [sc in each of next 2 sts, dec] around. (18 sc)

Round 13: [Sc in next st, dec] around. (12 sc)
Stuff.
Round 14: [Dec] around. (6 sc)

Fasten off and sew closed.

FROSTING

With cream yarn (HELLO 156)

Join in any of the front loops of Round 11 of the cake; [ch 2, sl st in next st] around. (24 ch-2 & 24 sl st) *(photos 1-4)*. Fasten off and weave in ends.

Embroidering Details
With pink (HELLO 109) and blue (HELLO 145) yarn and a needle, make some random stitches or French knots around the cake for decoration. *(photos 5-9)*

CANDLES (Make 6)

With pink yarn (HELLO 109) or blue yarn (HELLO 145) (3 of each color)

Ch 5, sl st in 2nd ch from hook, sl st in each of last 3 ch. (4 sl st)

Fasten off, leaving a long tail for sewing.

For the fire, use a little piece of gold yarn and add it to the top of the candle by looping it through the top stitch with the help of your hook. *(photos 10-16)*

Sew to the top of the cake.
(photos 17-18)

CAKE ASSEMBLY

1

2

3

27. GIFT 1

MATERIALS FOR GIFT 1

» Pink yarn (HELLO 109)
» Light blue yarn (HELLO 145)
» 2.5 mm hook
» Stuffing
» Yarn needle

With pink yarn (HELLO 109)

Round 1: Ch 5, sc in 2ⁿᵈ ch from hook, sc in each of next 2 ch, inc in last ch; working on other side of foundation ch, sc in each of next 3 ch, inc in last ch. (10 sc)

Round 2: [(3 sc) in next st, sc in each of next 2 sts, (3 sc) in next st, sc in next st st] 2 times. (18 sc)

Round 3: Working in **back loops** only, sc in each st around. (18 sc)

Round 4: Sc in each st around. (18 sc)

Round 5: Working in **back loops** only, [dec] around. (9 sc)

Stuff.

Fasten off and sew closed.

RIBBON

With light blue yarn (HELLO 145)
Ch 50.

Fasten off, wrap it around the gift, make a bow and trim the yarn tails. *(photos 1-4)*

Or, use a piece of yarn, wrap it around the gift and make a bow on top.

GIFT 1 ASSEMBLY

1

2

3
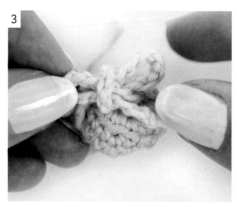

4

28. GIFT 2

MATERIALS FOR GIFT 2

» Yellow yarn (HELLO 120)
» Light blue yarn (HELLO 145)
» 2.5 mm hook
» Stuffing
» Yarn needle

With yellow yarn (HELLO 120)

Round 1: Make a magic ring, 8 sc in ring. (8 sc)

Round 2: [Sc in next st, (3 sc) in next st] around. (16 sc)

Round 3: Working in **back loops** only, sc in each st around. (16 sc)

Rounds 4-6: *(3 rounds)* Sc in each st around. (16 sc)

Round 7: Working in **back loops** only, [dec] around. (8 sc)

Stuff.

Fasten off and sew closed.

RIBBON

With light blue yarn (HELLO 145)

Ch 54.

Fasten off, wrap it around the gift, make a bow and trim the yarn tails. *(photo 1)*

Or, use a piece of yarn, wrap it around the gift and make a bow on top. *(photo 2)*

1

2

29. GARLAND

MATERIALS FOR GARLAND

» Light blue (HELLO 145)
» Pink yarn (HELLO 109)
» White yarn (HELLO 154)
» 2.5 mm hook
» Yarn needle

SCALLOPS (Make 6)

With light blue yarn (HELLO 145) or pink yarn (HELLO 109) (3 of each color)

Ch 4, (6 dc, ch 3, sl st) in 4th ch from hook.

Fasten off and weave in ends.

STRING

With white yarn (HELLO 154)

Ch 14, [join with a sc to right corner of a scallop, sc 4 more times along top of scallop, ch 4] 6 times, ch 14.
(photos 2-5)

Fasten off.

GARLAND ASSEMBLY

1

2
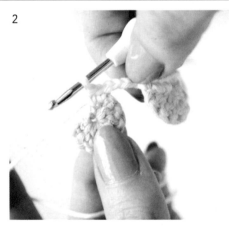

3
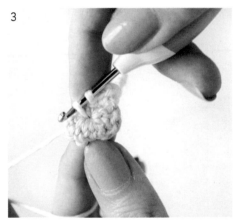

4
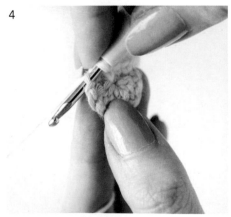

5

6
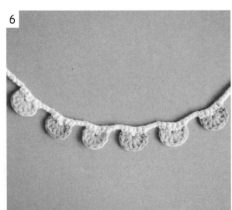

30. PARTY HATS

MATERIALS FOR PARTY HATS

» Light blue yarn (HELLO 145)
» 2.5 mm hook
» Yarn needle

With light blue yarn (HELLO 145)

Round 1: Make a magic ring, 4 sc in ring. (4 sc)

Round 2: [Inc in next st, sc in next st] around. (6 sc)

Round 3: Inc in next st, sc in each of next 5 sts. (7 sc)

Round 4: Sc in each of next 3 sts, inc in next st, sc in each of next 3 sts. (8 sc)

Round 5: Inc in next st, sc in each of next 7 sts. (9 sc)

Fasten off and weave in ends.

You can sew the hat on the head, or use a piece of yarn to make a strap so the hat is removable.

PARTY HATS

Gardener

31. GIRL
Finished Size
10.5 cm - 4 ¼"

32. DRESS
Finished Size
4 cm - 1 ½"

33. HAT
Finished Size
3.5 cm - 1 ⅜"

34. PLANT 1
Finished Size
5 cm - 2"

35. PLANT 2
Finished Size
3 cm - 1 ¼"

36. PLANT 3
Finished Size
4 cm - 1 ½"

37. PLANT 4
Finished Size
3 cm - 1 ¼"

38. BASKET
Finished Size
2 cm - ¾"

39. WATERING CAN
Finished Size
2.5 cm - 1"

31. GIRL

MATERIALS FOR GIRL

» Body color yarn (HELLO 162)
» Black yarn (HELLO 160)
» Brown yarn (HELLO 168)
» 2.5 mm hook
» Two 3 mm black beads & black thread or two 3 mm safety eyes
» Stuffing
» Yarn needle
» Pink embroidery floss & needle

LEGS & BODY

With body color yarn (HELLO 162)

You start by making the legs and then join them together and continue to the body.

Note: *If you want shoes, start each leg with brown yarn (HELLO 168) and switch to body color yarn after Round 3.*

First Leg

Round 1: Make a magic ring, 6 sc in ring. (6 sc)

Rounds 2-8: *(7 rounds)* Sc in each st around. (6 sc)

Fasten off, weave in ends and stuff the leg.

Second Leg + Body

Round 1: Make a magic ring, 6 sc in ring. (6 sc)

Rounds 2-8: *(7 rounds)* Sc in each st around. (6 sc)
Stuff.

Round 9: *(Joining Legs)* Sc in each of next 2 sts, attach with a sc to First Leg, sc in each of next 5 sts, sc in each of last 4 sts of Second Leg. (12 sc) *(photo 1)*

Round 10: [Sc in each of next 5 sts, inc in next st] around. (14 sc)

Rounds 11-15: *(5 rounds)* Sc in each st around. (14 sc)
Stuff.

Round 16: Sc in each of next 13 sts; end round here and move beginning of round marker to the last unworked st *(the next round will now start in this st)*. (14 sc)

Round 17: [Dec, sc in each of next 5 sts] around. (12 sc)

Round 18: [Dec, sc in each of next 4 sts] around. (10 sc)

Stuff a bit more.
Fasten off, leaving a long tail for sewing.

ARMS (Make 2)

With body color yarn (HELLO 162)

Round 1: Make a magic ring, 5 sc in ring. (5 sc)

Rounds 2-7: *(6 rounds)* Sc in each st around. (5 sc)

Do not stuff.

Fasten off, leaving a long tail for sewing. *(photo 2)*

HEAD

With body color yarn (HELLO 162)

Round 1: Ch 4, sc in 2nd ch from hook, sc in next ch, inc in last ch; working on other side of foundation ch, sc in each of next 2 ch, inc in last ch. (8 sc)

Round 2: [Inc in next st, sc in next st] around. (12 sc)

Round 3: Sc in next st, [inc in next st, sc in each of next 2 sts] 3 times, inc in next st, sc in next st. (16 sc)

Round 4: Sc in each of next 2 sts, inc in next st, [sc in each of next 3 sts, inc in next st] 3 times, sc in next st. (20 sc)

Round 5: [Sc in each of next 4 sts, inc in next st] around. (24 sc)

Rounds 6-10: *(5 rounds)* Sc in each st around. (24 sc)

Round 11: [Sc in each of next 2 sts, dec] around. (18 sc)

If you are using safety eyes, place them in now at Round 9, 5 sts apart.

Round 12: [Sc in next st, dec] around. (12 sc)

Stuff.

Round 13: [Dec] around. (6 sc)

Fasten off and sew closed. *(photo 3)*
Sew the head to the body.

HAIR

With black yarn (HELLO 160)

Round 1: Ch 5, hdc in 3rd ch from hook, hdc in next ch, (2 hdc) in last ch; working on other side of foundation ch, hdc in each of next 2 ch, (2 hdc) in last ch; join with sl st to first hdc. (8 hdc)

Round 2: Ch 2, [hdc in next st, (2 hdc) in next st] around; join with sl st to first hdc. (12 hdc)

Round 3: Ch 2, [hdc in next st, (2 hdc) in next st] around; join with sl st to first hdc. (18 hdc)

Round 4: Ch 2, [hdc in each of next 3 sts, (2 hdc) in next st] 4 times, hdc in each of next 2 sts; join with sl st to first hdc. (22 hdc)

Round 5: Ch 2, hdc in each st around; join with sl st to first hdc. (22 hdc)

Round 6: Hdc in each of next 15 sts, sc in each of next 2 sts, (2 hdc) in each of next 2 sts, sl st in next st, (2 hdc) in next st, (hdc, sl st) in next st. (23 hdc, 2 sc, 2 sl st)

Round 7: Ch 1, sc in next st, hdc in each of next 12 sts, sc in next st, ch 1, sl st in next st; end round here.

Fasten off, leaving a long tail for sewing. *(photo 4)*

Pigtails

Round 1: Make a magic ring, 5 sc in the ring. (5 sc)

Round 2: Inc in each st around. (10 sc)

Round 3: Sc in each st around. (10 sc)

Round 4: [Dec] around. (5 sc)

Round 5: Sc in each st around. (5 sc) *(photo 5)*
Fasten off, leaving a long tail for sewing. Do not stuff.

Quick Assembly Guide

Eyes: Round 9 of head, 5 sts apart

Mouth: Embroider between eyes

Cheeks: Embroider under eyes

Hair: On top of the head

Pigtails: On either side of head, at hairline.

Arms: Round 17 of body

GIRL ASSEMBLY

1 Legs

2 Body Arms

3 Head

4 Hair

5

6

7

8

32. DRESS

MATERIALS FOR DRESS

» Green yarn (HELLO 172)
» 2.5 mm hook
» Yarn needle

With green yarn (HELLO 172)

Row 1: Ch 22, sc in 2nd ch from hook, sc in each of next 2 ch; *(First Arm Hole)* ch 4, skip next 4 ch of ch-22, sc in each of next 7 ch of ch-22; *(Second Arm Hole)* ch 4, skip next 4 ch of ch-22, sc in each of next 3 ch of ch-22. (13 sc & 2 ch-4) *(photos 1-3)*

Row 2: Ch 1, turn, sc in each of next 3 sts; working in ch-4, sc in each of next 4 ch, sc in each of next 7 sts; working in ch-4, sc in each of next 4 ch, sc in each of next 3 sts. (21 sc)

Rows 3-5: *(3 rows)* Ch 1, turn, sc in each st across. (21 sc)

Row 6: Ch 1, turn; working in **back loops** only, [sc in each of next 2 sts, inc in next st] across. (28 sc)

Rows 7-9: *(3 rows)* Ch 1, turn, sc in each st across. (28 sc)

Fasten off, leaving a long tail for sewing.
Place the dress on the girl and whipstitch the edges together. *(photo 5)*

DRESS ASSEMBLY

1

2

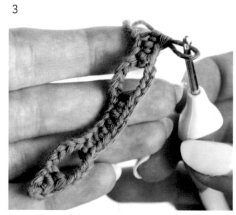

3

4

5

6

33. HAT

MATERIALS FOR HAT

» Dark beige yarn (HELLO 125)
» 2.5 mm hook
» Yarn needle

With dark beige yarn (HELLO 125)

Round 1: Make a magic ring, ch 2, 8 hdc in ring; join with sl st to first hdc. (8 hdc)

Round 2: Ch 2, (2 hdc) in each st around; join with sl st to first hdc. (16 hdc)

Round 3: Ch 2, [hdc in next st, (2 hdc) in next st] around; join with sl st to first hdc. (24 hdc)

Round 4: Ch 2, [hdc in each of next 2 sts, (2 hdc) in next st] around; join with sl st to first hdc. (32 hdc)

Rounds 5-6: *(2 rounds)* Ch 2, hdc in each st around; join with sl st to first hdc. (32 hdc)

Round 7: Ch 2; working in **front loops** only, [(2 hdc) in next st, hdc in each of next 3 sts] around; join with sl st to first hdc. (40 hdc)

Round 8: Ch 2, [(2 hdc) in next st, hdc in each of next 4 sts] around; join with sl st to first hdc. (48 hdc)
Fasten off and weave in ends.

34. PLANT 1

MATERIALS FOR PLANT 1

» Terracotta yarn (HELLO 166)
» Bright green yarn (HELLO 171)
» 2.5 mm hook
» Yarn needle

POT

With terracotta yarn (HELLO 166)

Round 1: Make a magic ring, 6 sc in ring. (6 sc)

Round 2: Inc in each st around. (12 sc)

Round 3: Working in **back loops** only, sc in each st around. (12 sc)

Rounds 4-5: *(2 rounds)* Sc in each st around. (12 sc)

Fasten off and weave in ends.

LEAVES

1st Leaf

With bright green yarn (HELLO 171)

Ch 10, sl st in 2nd ch from hook, sc in next ch, hdc in next ch, dc in each of next 4 ch, hdc in next ch, (sc, sl st) in next ch, ch 4, sc in 2nd ch from hook, sl st each of next 2 ch; working on other side of ch-10 foundation ch, (sl st, hdc) in next ch, hdc in next ch, dc in each of next 4 ch, hdc in next ch, sc in next ch, sl st in last ch.

Fasten off and weave in ends.

2nd Leaf

With bright green yarn (HELLO 171)

Ch 10, sl st in 2nd ch from hook, sc in next ch, hdc in next ch, dc in each of next 4 ch, hdc in next ch, (sc, sl st) in next ch, ch 7, sc in 2nd ch from hook, sl st in each of next 5 ch; working on other side of ch-10 foundation ch, (sl st, hdc) in next ch, hdc in next ch, dc in each of next 4 ch, hdc in next ch, sc in next ch, sl st in last ch.

Fasten off and weave in ends.

3rd Leaf

With bright green yarn (HELLO 171)

Ch 10, sl st in 2nd ch from hook, sc in next ch, hdc in next ch, dc in each of next 4 ch, hdc in next ch, (sc, sl st) in next ch, ch 6, sc in 2nd ch from hook, sl st in each of next 4 ch; working on other side of ch-10 foundation ch, (sl st, hdc) in next ch, hdc in next ch, dc in each of next 4 ch, hdc in next ch, sc in next ch, sl st in last ch.

Fasten off, leaving a long tail for sewing.

Sew all the stems together, then secure the plant to the bottom of the pot by sewing it in place.

PLANT 1 ASSEMBLY

35. PLANT 2

MATERIALS FOR PLANT 2

» Terracotta yarn (HELLO 166)
» Light green yarn (HELLO 169)
» 2.5 mm hook
» Yarn needle

POT

With terracotta yarn (HELLO 166)

Round 1: Make a magic ring, 6 sc in ring. (6 sc)

Round 2: Inc in each st around. (12 sc)

Round 3: Working in **back loops** only, sc in each st around. (12 sc)

Rounds 4-5: *(2 rounds)* Sc in each st around. (12 sc)
Fasten off and weave in ends.

LEAVES

With light green yarn (HELLO 169)

(Leaf 1) Ch 7, sl st in 2nd ch from hook, sc in next ch, sl st in each of next 4 ch;
(Leaf 2) ch 8, sl st in 2nd ch from hook, sc in next ch, sl st in each of next 5 ch;
(Leaf 3) ch 7, sl st in 2nd ch from hook, sc in next ch, sl st in each of next 4 ch;
(Leaf 4) ch 9, sl st in 2nd ch from hook, sc in next ch, sl st in each of next 6 ch;
(Leaf 5) ch 7, sl st in 2nd ch from hook, sc in next ch, sl st in each of next 4 ch.

Fasten off with a long tail and secure the plant to the bottom of the pot by sewing it in place.

PLANT 2 ASSEMBLY

36. PLANT 3

MATERIALS FOR PLANT 3

» Terracotta yarn (HELLO 166)
» Dark green yarn (HELLO 135)
» White yarn (HELLO 154)
» Yellow yarn (HELLO 120)
» 2.5 mm hook
» Yarn needle

POT

With terracotta yarn (HELLO 166)

Round 1: Make a magic ring, 6 sc in ring. (6 sc)

Round 2: Inc in each st around. (12 sc)

Round 3: Working in **back loops** only, sc in each st around. (12 sc)

Rounds 4-5: *(2 rounds)* Sc in each st around. (12 sc)

Fasten off and weave in ends.

FLOWER

With white yarn (HELLO 154)

Make a magic ring, [ch 4, sl st in 2nd ch from hook, sc in each of next 2 ch, sl st in ring] 5 times.
Fasten off and weave in ends.

Tie a short strand of yellow yarn to the center of the flower to create a couple stamens.

STEM

With dark green yarn (HELLO 135)

Ch 6, sl st in 2nd ch from hook, sl st in each of next 4 ch.

Fasten off, leaving a long tail for sewing.

Sew the flower on the stem.

LEAF (Make 3)

With dark green yarn (HELLO 135)

Ch 5, sl st in 2nd ch from hook, sc in next ch, hdc in next ch, (dc, sl st) in next ch, ch 5, sl st in 2nd ch from hook, sl st in each of next 3 ch; working on other side of first ch-5 foundation ch, (sl st, ch 1, dc) in next ch, hdc in next ch, sc in next ch, sl st in last ch.

Fasten off and weave in ends for the first two leaves. For the last leaf, fasten off, leaving a long tail for sewing.

Sew the leaves and stem together, then secure the plant to the bottom of the pot by sewing it in place.

PLANT 3 ASSEMBLY

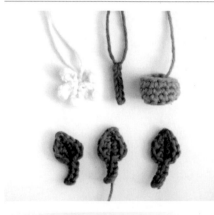

37. PLANT 4

MATERIALS FOR PLANT 4

» Terracotta yarn (HELLO 166)
» Green yarn (HELLO 169)
» White yarn (HELLO 154)
» Yellow yarn (HELLO 120)
» 2.5 mm hook
» Yarn needle

POT

With terracotta yarn (HELLO 166)

Round 1: Ch 4, sc in 2nd ch from hook, sc in next ch, inc in last ch; working on other side of foundation ch, sc in each of next 2 ch, inc in last ch. (8 sc)

Round 2: [Inc in next st, sc in next st] around. (12 sc)

Round 3: Working in **back loops** only, sc in each st around. (12 sc)

Rounds 4-5: (2 rounds) Sc in each st around. (12 sc)

Fasten off and weave in ends.

PLANT

With green yarn (HELLO 169)

Round 1: Ch 4, sc in 2nd ch from hook, sc in next ch, inc in last ch; working on other side of foundation ch, sc in each of next 2 ch, inc in last ch. (8 sc)

Round 2: [Inc in next st, sc in next st] around. (12 sc)

Rounds 3-4: (2 rounds) Sc in each st around. (12 sc)

Round 5: [Sc in each of next 4 sts, dec] around. (10 sc)

Rounds 6-7: (2 rounds) Sc in each st around. (10 sc)
Stuff.

Round 8: [Dec] around. (5 sc)
Fasten off and sew closed.

FLOWER

With white yarn (HELLO 154)

Make a magic ring, [ch 2, sl st in ring] 5 times.

Fasten off, leaving a long tail for sewing.

Use a piece of yellow yarn to make a french knot in the middle of the flower. Sew the flower on the plant, then place the plant within the pot.

PLANT 4 ASSEMBLY

38. BASKET

MATERIALS FOR BASKET

» Cinnamon yarn (HELLO 166)

» 2.5 mm hook

» Yarn needle

With cinnamon yarn (HELLO 166)

Round 1: Ch 4, sc in 2nd ch from hook, sc in next ch, inc in last ch; working on other side of foundation ch, sc in each of next 2 ch, inc in last ch. (8 sc)

Round 2: [Inc in next st, sc in next st] around. (12 sc)

Round 3: Sc in next st, inc in next st, [sc in each of next 2 sts, inc in next st] 3 times, sc in last st. (16 sc)

Round 4: Working in **back loops** only, sc in each st around. (16 sc)

Rounds 5-6: *(2 rounds)* Sc in each st around. (16 sc)

Fasten off and weave in ends.

Handle

With cinnamon yarn (HELLO 166)

Join to a st in the middle of one of the long sides of Round 6; ch 11, sl st in 2nd ch from hook, sl st in each of next 9 ch. *(photos 1-2)*

Fasten off, leaving a long tail for sewing.

Sew the free end of the handle to the middle of the opposite long side of Round 6. *(photo 3)*

BASKET ASSEMBLY

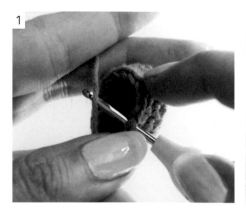

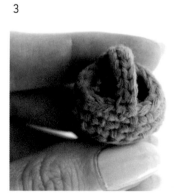

39. WATERING CAN

MATERIALS FOR WATERING CAN

» Light blue yarn (HELLO 145)

» 2.5 mm hook

» Yarn needle

With light blue yarn (HELLO 145)

Round 1: Make a magic ring, 6 sc in ring. (6 sc)

Round 2: Inc in each st around. (12 sc)

Round 3: Working in **back loops** only, sc in each st around. (12 sc)

Rounds 4-6: *(3 rounds)* Sc in each st around. (12 sc)

Next, you will continue by making the top handle and then the side handle. *(Top Handle)* Sl st in next st, ch 6, skip next 5 sts, sl st in next st *(Top Handle attached; photos 1-2); (Side Handle)* Sl st in each of next 3 sts, ch 8, sl st in 2nd ch from hook, sl st in each of next 6 ch, sl st in the same st the ch-8 starts from, sl st in each of next 2 sts. *(photo 3)*

Fasten off, leaving a long tail, and sew the free end of the side handle to the bottom of the watering can. *(photos 4-5)*

SPOUT

With light blue yarn (HELLO 145)

Ch 5, sc in 2nd ch from hook, sc in each of next 3 ch.

Fasten off, leaving a long tail for sewing.

Sew along the long edges (whipstitch) to form a long cylinder.

Quick Assembly Guide

Spout: Round 3

WATERING CAN ASSEMBLY

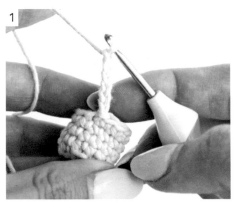

1

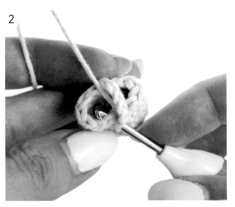

2

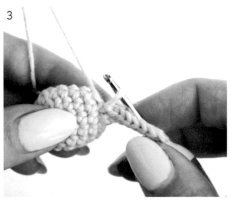

3

4

5

Explorer

40. EXPLORER BOY
Finished Size
10 cm - 4"

41. OVERALLS
Finished Size
5 cm - 2"

42. HAT
Finished Size
2.5 cm - 1"

43. BINOCULARS
Finished Size
5.5 cm - 2 ¼"

44. EXPLORER'S MAP
Finished Size
3 cm - 1 ¼"

45. BACKPACK
Finished Size
3.5 cm - 1 ⅜"

40. EXPLORER BOY

MATERIALS FOR EXPLORER BOY

» Body color yarn (HELLO 162)
» Black yarn (HELLO 160)
» White yarn (HELLO 154)
» 2.5 mm hook
» Two 3 mm black beads & black thread or two 3 mm safety eyes
» Stuffing
» Yarn needle
» Pink embroidery floss & needle

LEGS & BODY

With body color yarn (HELLO 162)

You start by making the legs and then join them together and continue to the body.

Note: *If you want shoes, start each leg with black yarn (HELLO 160) and switch to body color yarn after Round 3.*

First Leg

Round 1: Make a magic ring, 6 sc in ring. (6 sc)

Rounds 2-8: *(7 rounds)* Sc in each st around. (6 sc)

Fasten off, weave in ends and stuff the leg.

Second Leg + Body

Round 1: Make a magic ring, 6 sc in ring. (6 sc)

Rounds 2-8: *(7 rounds)* Sc in each st around. (6 sc)

Stuff.

Change to white yarn (HELLO 154)

Round 9: *(Joining Legs)* Sc in each of next 2 sts, attach with a sc to First Leg, sc in each of next 5 sts, sc in each of last 4 sts of Second Leg. (12 sc) *(photo 1)*

Round 10: [Sc in each of next 5 sts, inc in next st] around. (14 sc)

Rounds 11-15: *(5 rounds)* Sc in each st around. (14 sc)

Stuff.

Round 16: Sc in each of next 13 sts; end round here and move beginning of round marker to the last unworked st *(the next round will now start in this st)*. (14 sc)

Round 17: [Dec, sc in each of next 5 sts] around. (12 sc)

Round 18: [Dec, sc in each of next 4 sts] around. (10 sc)

Stuff a bit more.

Fasten off, leaving a long tail for sewing.

ARMS (Make 2)

With body color yarn (HELLO 162)

Round 1: Make a magic ring, 5 sc in the ring. (5 sc)

Round 2: Sc in each st around. (5 sc)

Change to white yarn (HELLO 154)

Rounds 3-7: *(5 rounds)* Sc in each st around. (5 sc)

Do not stuff.

Fasten off, leaving a long tail for sewing.

HEAD

With body color yarn (HELLO 162)

Round 1: Ch 4, sc in 2nd ch from hook, sc in next ch, inc in last ch; working on other side of foundation ch, sc in each of next 2 ch, inc in last ch. (8 sc)

Round 2: [Inc in next st, sc in next st] around. (12 sc)

Round 3: Sc in next st, [inc in next st, sc in each of next 2 sts] 3 times, inc in next st, sc in next st. (16 sc)

Round 4: Sc in each of next 2 sts, inc in next st, [sc in each of next 3 sts, inc in next st] 3 times, sc in next st. (20 sc)

Round 5: [Sc in each of next 4 sts, inc in next st] around. (24 sc)

Rounds 6-10: *(5 rounds)* Sc in each st around. (24 sc)

Round 11: [Sc in each of next 2 sts, dec] around. (18 sc)

If you are using safety eyes, place them in now at Round 9, 5 sts apart.

Round 12: [Sc in next st, dec] around. (12 sc)

Stuff.

Round 13: [Dec] around. (6 sc)

Fasten off and sew closed. *(photo 2)* Sew the head to the body.

HAIR

With black yarn (HELLO 160)

Round 1: Ch 5, hdc in 3rd ch from hook, hdc in next ch, (2 hdc) in last ch; working on other side of foundation ch, hdc in each of next 2 ch, (2 hdc) in last ch; join with sl st to first hdc. (8 hdc)

Round 2: Ch 2, [hdc in next st, (2 hdc) in next st] around; join with sl st to first hdc. (12 hdc)

Round 3: Ch 2, [hdc in next st, (2 hdc) in next st] around; join with sl st to first hdc. (18 hdc)

Round 4: Ch 2, [hdc in each of next 3 sts, (2 hdc) in next st] 4 times, hdc in each of last 2 sts; join with sl st to first hdc. (22 hdc)

Round 5: Ch 2, hdc in each st around; join with sl st to first hdc. (22 hdc)

Round 6: Hdc in each of next 15 sts, sc in each of next 2 sts, (2 hdc) in each of next 2 sts, sl st in next st, (2 hdc) in next st, (hdc, sl st) in next st. (23 hdc, 2 sc, 2 sl st)

Round 7: Ch 1, sc in next st, hdc in each of next 12 sts, sc in next st, ch 1, sl st in next st; end round here.

Fasten off, leaving a long tail for sewing. *(photo 3)*

Quick Assembly Guide

Eyes: Round 9 of head, 5 sts apart
Mouth: Embroider between eyes
Cheeks: Embroider under eyes
Hair: On top of the head
Arms: Round 17 of body

EXPLORER BOY ASSEMBLY

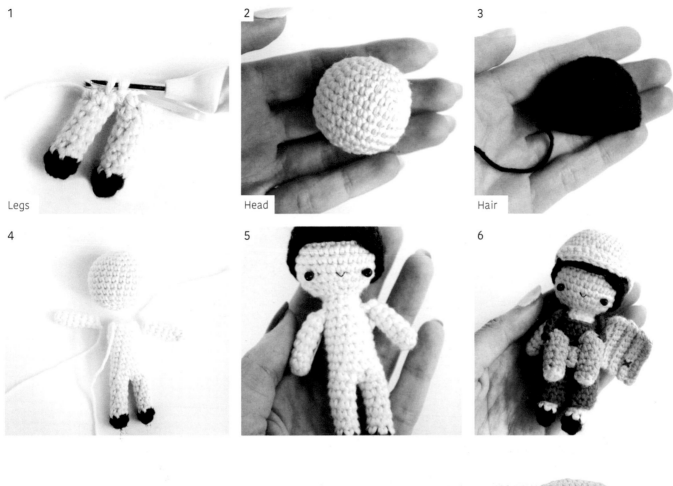

1

Legs

2

Head

3

Hair

4

5

6

41. OVERALLS

MATERIALS FOR OVERALLS

» Blue yarn (HELLO 150)
» 2.5 mm hook
» Yarn needle

With blue yarn (HELLO 150)

You will start by making each pant leg and then join them together and continue to the body of the overalls.

1st Pant Leg

Round 1: Ch 10; join with sl st in first ch to form a ring; ch 1, sc in each ch around; join with sl st to first sc. (10 sc)

Rounds 2-3: *(2 rounds)* Ch 1, sc in each st around; join with sl st to first sc. (10 sc)

Fasten off and weave in ends.

2nd Pant Leg

Round 1: Ch 10; join with sl st in first ch to form a ring; ch 1, sc in each ch around; join with sl st to first sc. (10 sc)

Rounds 2-3: *(2 rounds)* Ch 1, sc in each st around; join with sl st to first sc. (10 sc)

Round 4: *(Joining Pant Legs)* Ch 1, sc in each of next 2 sts, attach with a single crochet to 1st Pant Leg, sc in each of next 9 sts, sc in each of last 8 sts of 2nd Pant Leg; join with sl st to first sc. (20 sc)

Rounds 5-8: *(4 Rounds)* Ch 1, sc in each st around; join with sl st to first sc. (20 sc)

Round 9: Ch 1, sc in each of next 7 sts, dec, sc in each of next 8 sts, dec, sc in next st; join with sl st to first sc. (18 sc)

You will now start working in rows to create the bib.

Row 10: Ch 1, sc in each of next 6 sts. (6 sc)

Rows 11-12: *(2 rows)* Ch 1, turn, sc in each of next 6 sts. (6 sc)

Next, you will continue by making the shoulder straps.

Ch 8, skip next 4 sts of Round 9, join with sl st to next st *(photo 1)*, sl st in each of next 3 sts *(photo 2)*, ch 8 *(photo 3)*, join with sl st to top right corner of bib *(photo 4)*.

Fasten off and weave in ends.

OVERALLS ASSEMBLY

1

2

3

4

42. HAT

MATERIALS FOR HAT

» Light blue yarn (HELLO 145)

» 2.5 mm hook

» Yarn needle

With light blue yarn (HELLO 145)

Round 1: Make a magic ring, 7 sc in ring. (7 sc)

Round 2: Inc in each st around. (14 sc)

Round 3: [Sc in next st, inc in next st] around. (21 sc)

Round 4: [Sc in each of next 2 sts, inc in next st] around. (28 sc)

Rounds 5-8: *(4 rounds)* Sc in each st around. (28 sc)

Round 9: Sc in each st around; join with sl st to first sc. (28 sc)

You will now start working in rows to create the brim.

Row 10: Working in **front loops** only, ch 1, sc in each of next 4 sts, inc in next st, sc in each of next 4 sts, sl st in next st. (10 sc & sl st)

Row 11: Ch 1, turn, skip sl st, sc in each of next 4 sts, inc in next st, sc in each of next 4 sts, sl st in next st. (10 sc & sl st)

Row 12: Ch 1, turn, skip sl st, sc In each of next 4 sts, dec, sc in each of next 3 sts, sl st in next st. (8 sc & sl st)

Fasten off and weave in ends.

43. BINOCULARS

MATERIALS FOR BINOCULARS

» Light blue yarn (HELLO 145)
» Gray yarn (HELLO 159)
» Brown yarn (HELLO 168)
» 2.5 mm hook
» Yarn needle

BARRELS (Make 2)

With light blue yarn (HELLO 145)

Round 1: Make a magic ring, 6 sc in ring. (6 sc)

Change to gray yarn (HELLO 159)

Round 2: Working in **back loops** only, sc in each st around. (6 sc)

Rounds 3-7: *(5 rounds)* Sc in each st around. (6 sc)

Fasten off and sew closed.

MIDDLE PIECE

With gray yarn (HELLO 159)

Row 1: Ch 4, sc in 2nd ch from hook, sc in each of next 2 ch. (3 sc)

Row 2: Ch 1, turn, sc in each st across. (3 sc)

Fasten off, leaving a long tail for sewing.

Fold the piece in half and sew the halves together. *(photo 1)*

Sew the Middle Piece between the two Barrels. *(photos 2-4)*

STRAP

With brown yarn (HELLO 168)

Leave a long tail and ch 24.

Fasten off, leaving a long tail for sewing.

Sew each end to the sides of the binoculars. *(photo 5)*

BINOCULARS ASSEMBLY

1

2

3

4

5

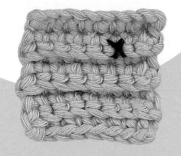

MATERIALS FOR EXPLORER'S MAP

- » Beige yarn (HELLO 158)
- » Red yarn (HELLO 114)
- » 2.5 mm hook
- » Yarn needle

With beige yarn (HELLO 158)

Row 1: Ch 9, sc in 2nd ch from hook, sc in each of next 7 ch. (8 sc)

Rows 2-7: *(6 rows)* Working in **back loops** only, ch 1, turn, sc in each of next 8 sts. (8 sc)

Fasten off and weave in ends.

With red yarn (HELLO 114), stitch an 'x' anywhere on the map.

45. BACKPACK

MATERIALS FOR BACKPACK

» Green yarn (HELLO 172)

» 2.5 mm hook

» Yarn needle

With green yarn (HELLO 172)

Round 1: Ch 5, sc in 2nd ch from hook, sc in each of next 2 ch, inc in last ch; working on other side of foundation ch, sc in each of next 3 ch, inc in last ch. (10 sc)

Round 2: [Inc in next st, sc in each of next 2 sts, inc in next st, sc in next st] around. (14 sc)

Rounds 3-8: *(6 rounds)* Sc in each st around. (14 sc)

You will now start working in rows to create the flap.

Row 9: Working in **front loops** only, ch 1, turn, sc in each of next 6 sts. (6 sc)

Rows 10-11: *(2 rows)* Ch 1, turn, sc in each of next 6 sts. (6 sc)

Row 12: Ch 1, turn, dec, sc in each of next 2 sts, dec. (4 sc)

Row 13: Ch 1, turn, [dec] 2 times. (2 sc)

Continue from here to make the fastening.

Ch 5, sl st in same st the ch-5 comes from.

Fasten off and weave in ends.

STRAPS

With green yarn (HELLO 172)

Leaving a long tail, ch 14; join with a sl st in 2nd back loop *(from right)* of Round 8, sl st in next back loop, ch 7, sl st in each of next 2 back loops, ch 14. *(photos 1-3)*

Fasten off, leaving a long tail for sewing.

Using the two long tails, sew the straps on the bottom of the backpack. *(photo 4)*

1

2

3

4

Sheep

46. BABY SHEEP
Finished Size
5.5 cm - 2 ¼"

47. SHEEP MUM
Finished Size
9.5 cm - 3 ¾"

46. BABY SHEEP

MATERIALS FOR BABY SHEEP

» Gray yarn (HELLO 174)
» Dark gray yarn (HELLO 159)
» Light cream yarn (HELLO 155)
» 2.5 mm hook
» Two 3 mm black beads & black thread or two 3 mm safety eyes
» Stuffing
» Yarn needle
» Pink embroidery floss & needle

BODY & HEAD

With gray yarn (HELLO 174)

Round 1: Make a magic ring, 6 sc in ring. (6 sc)

Round 2: Inc in each st around. (12 sc)

Round 3: [Sc in next st, inc in next st] around. (18 sc)

Round 4: Working in **back loops** only, sc in each st around. (18 sc)

Rounds 5-7: *(3 rounds)* Sc in each st around. (18 sc)

Round 8: [Dec, sc in next st] around. (12 sc)

Round 9: Inc in each st around. (24 sc)

Rounds 10-14: *(5 rounds)* Sc in each st around. (24 sc)

If you are using safety eyes, place them in now at Round 11, 5 sts apart.

Round 15: [Dec, sc in each of next 2 sts] around. (18 sc)

Stuff.

Round 16: [Dec, sc in next st] around. (12 sc)

Round 17: [Dec] around. (6 sc)
Fasten off and sew closed.

BELLY

With light cream yarn (HELLO 155)

Round 1: Make a magic ring, ch 2, 8 hdc in ring; join with sl st to first hdc. (8 hdc)

Fasten off, leaving a long tail for sewing.

ARMS & LEGS (Make 4)

With gray yarn (HELLO 174)
Ch 3, hdc in 3rd ch from hook.
Fasten off, leaving a long tail for sewing.

HAIR

With dark gray yarn (HELLO 159)

Round 1: Make a magic ring, ch 2, 8 hdc in ring; join with sl st to first hdc. (8 hdc)

Round 2: [Ch 2, sl st in next st] around. Fasten off, leaving a long tail for sewing.

EARS (Make 2)

With gray yarn (HELLO 174)

Round 1: Make a magic ring, 6 sc in ring. (6 sc)

Rounds 2-4: *(3 rounds)* Sc in each st around. (6 sc)

Fasten off, leaving a long tail for sewing.

Do not stuff.

Quick Assembly Guide

Eyes: Round 11, 5 sts apart

Cheeks: Embroider under eyes

Nose: Embroider between eyes

Ears: Round 17, on the sides

Arms: Rounds 7-8, 6 sts apart

Legs: Round 4, 2 sts apart

Hair: On top of head

Belly: Rounds 5-7 of body

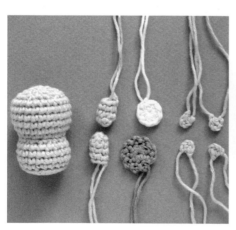

47. SHEEP MUM

MATERIALS FOR SHEEP MUM

- » Gray yarn (HELLO 174)
- » Dark gray yarn (HELLO 159)
- » Light cream yarn (HELLO 155)
- » 2.5 mm hook
- » Two 4 mm black beads & black thread or two 4 mm safety eyes
- » Stuffing
- » Yarn needle
- » Pink embroidery floss & needle

*special stitch: Popcorn Stitch - (4 dc) in next st, remove hook, insert hook from front to back into the 1st dc, grab the working loop with hook, pull loop through the dc, ch 1.

HEAD

With gray yarn (HELLO 174)

Round 1: Make a magic ring, 6 sc in ring. (6 sc)

Round 2: Inc in each st around. (12 sc)

Round 3: [Sc in next st, inc in next st] around. (18 sc)

Round 4: [Sc in each of next 2 sts, inc in next st] around. (24 sc)

Round 5: [Sc in each of next 3 sts, inc in next st] around. (30 sc)

Round 6: [Sc in each of next 4 sts, inc in next st] around. (36 sc)

Rounds 7-13: *(7 rounds)* Sc in each st around. (36 sc)

If you are using safety eyes, place them in now at Round 10, 7 sts apart.

Round 14: [Dec, sc in each of next 4 sts] around. (30 sc)

Round 15: [Dec, sc in each of next 3 sts] around. (24 sc)

Round 16: [Dec, sc in each of next 2 sts] around. (18 sc)

Stuff.

Round 17: [Dec, sc in next st] around. (12 sc)

Round 18: [Dec] around. (6 sc)

Fasten off and sew closed.

HAIR

With dark gray yarn (HELLO 159)

Round 1: Make a magic ring, 6 sc in ring. (6 sc)

Round 2: Inc in each st around. (12 sc)

Round 3: Make a popcorn stitch in each st around. (12 popcorn stitches)

Fasten off, leaving a long tail for sewing. *(photo 1)*

EARS

With gray yarn (HELLO 174)

Round 1: Make a magic ring, 6 sc in ring. (6 sc)

Round 2: [Sc in each of next 2 sts, inc in next st] around. (8 sc)

Rounds 3-6: *(4 rounds)* Sc in each st around. (8 sc)

Round 7: [Dec, sc in each of next 2 sts] around. (6 sc)

Fasten off, leaving a long tail for sewing.

Stuff just a bit.

BODY

With gray yarn (HELLO 174)

Round 1: Make a magic ring, 6 sc in ring. (6 sc)

Round 2: Inc in each st around. (12 sc)

Round 3: [Sc in next st, inc in next st] around. (18 sc)

Round 4: [Sc in each of next 2 sts, inc in next st] around. (24 sc)

Round 5: Sc in each of next 4 sts, [sc in next st, inc in next st] 4 times, sc in each of next 4 sts, [sc in next st, inc in next st] 4 times. (32 sc)

Round 6: Working in **back loops** only, sc in each st around. (32 sc)

Rounds 7-12: *(6 rounds)* Sc in each st around. (32 sc)

Round 13: [Sc in each of next 4 sts, dec] 5 times, sc in each of last 2 sts. (27 sc)

Round 14: [Sc in each of next 4 sts, dec] 4 times, sc in each of last 3 sts. (23 sc)

Round 15: [Sc in each of next 5 sts, dec] 3 times, sc in each of last 2 sts (20 sc)

Fasten off, leaving a long tail for sewing.

Stuff.

Sew the head to the body.

ARMS & LEGS (Make 4)

With gray yarn (HELLO 174)

Ch 4, hdc in 3rd ch from hook, (2 hdc) in last ch; working on other side of foundation ch, (2 hdc) in next ch, hdc in last ch. (6 hdc)

Fasten off, leaving a long tail for sewing.

BELLY

With light cream yarn (HELLO 155)

Round 1: Make a magic ring, ch 3, 14 dc in ring; join with sl st to first dc. (14 dc)

Fasten off, leaving a long tail for sewing.

Quick Assembly Guide

Eyes: Round 10 of head, 7 sts apart

Cheeks: Embroider under eyes

Nose: Embroider between eyes

Ears: Rounds 4-5 of head, on the sides

Arms: Rounds 11-13 of body, 17 sts apart

Legs: Round 5 of body, 2 sts apart

Hair: Sew on top of the head

Belly: Rounds 7-12 of body

1

Hair

Hair

Miniatures

48. LEAF
Finished Size
5.5 cm - 2 ¼"

49. DROP
Finished Size
3.5 cm - 1 ⅜"

50. BLUEBERRY
Finished Size
3 cm - 1 ¼"

51. FLOWER
Finished Size
3 cm - 1 ¼"

52. MUSHROOM SMALL
Finished Size
3.5 cm - 1 ⅜"

53. MUSHROOM BIG
Finished Size
4 cm - 1 ½"

48. LEAF

MATERIALS FOR LEAF

- » Green yarn (HELLO 171)
- » 2.5 mm hook
- » Two 2 mm black beads & black thread or two 3 mm safety eyes
- » Stuffing
- » Yarn needle
- » Pink embroidery floss & needle

With green yarn (HELLO 171)

Round 1: Make a magic ring, 5 sc in ring. (5 sc)

Round 2: Inc in next st, sc in each of next 4 sts. (6 sc)

Round 3: Inc in next st, sc in each of next 5 sts. (7 sc)

Round 4: [Inc in next st, sc in next st] 3 times, inc in last st. (11 sc)

Round 5: [Inc in next st, sc in each of next 2 sts] 3 times, inc in next st, sc in last st. (15 sc)

Round 6: [Inc in next st, sc in each of next 3 sts] 3 times, inc in next st, sc in each of last 2 sts. (19 sc)

Rounds 7-9: *(3 rounds)* Sc in each st around. (19 sc)

Round 10: [Dec, sc in each of next 4 sts] 3 times, sc in last st. (16 sc)

If you are using safety eyes, place them in now at Round 8, 3 sts apart.

Round 11: [Dec, sc in each of next 3 sts] 3 times, sc in last st. (13 sc)

Round 12: [Dec, sc in each of next 2 sts]

3 times, sc in last st. (10 sc)

Stuff.

Round 13: [Dec] around. (5 sc)

Rounds 14-15: *(2 rounds)* Sc in each st around. (5 sc)

Fasten off and sew closed.

Quick Assembly Guide

Eyes: Round 8, 3 sts apart

Smile: Embroider between eyes

Cheeks: Embroider under eyes

49. DROP

MATERIALS FOR DROP

» Light blue yarn (HELLO 148)
» 2.5 mm hook
» Two 2 mm black beads & black thread or two 3 mm safety eyes
» Stuffing
» Yarn needle
» Pink embroidery floss & needle

With light blue yarn (HELLO 148)

Round 1: Make a magic ring, 7 sc in ring. (7 sc)

Round 2: Inc in each st around. (14 sc)

Round 3: [Sc in each of next 2 sts, inc in next st] 4 times, sc in each of last 2 sts. (18 sc)

Rounds 4-6: *(3 rounds)* Sc in each st around. (18 sc)
If you are using safety eyes, place them in now at Round 4, 3 sts apart.

Round 7: [Dec, sc in next st] around. (12 sc)

Round 8: [Dec, sc in next st] around. (8 sc)

Round 9: Sc in each st around. (8 sc)

Stuff.

Round 10: [Dec, sc in next st] 2 times, dec. (5 sc)
Fasten off and sew closed.

Quick Assembly Guide

Eyes: Round 4, 3 sts apart
Smile: Embroider between eyes
Cheeks: Embroider under eyes

50. BLUEBERRY

MATERIALS FOR BLUEBERRY

» Blue yarn (HELLO 148)
» 2.5 mm hook
» Two 2 mm black beads & black thread or two 3 mm safety eyes
» Stuffing
» Yarn needle
» Pink embroidery floss & needle

With blue yarn (HELLO 148)

Round 1: Make a magic ring, 6 sc in ring. (6 sc)

Round 2: Inc in each st around. (12 sc)

Round 3: [Sc in next st, inc in next st] around. (18 sc)

Rounds 4-6: (3 rounds) Sc in each st around. (18 sc) If you are using safety eyes, place them in now at Round 4, 3 sts apart.

Round 7: [Dec, sc in next st] around. (12 sc)
Stuff.

Round 8: [Dec] around. (6 sc)

Round 9: Sc in each st around. (6 sc)

Round 10: Working in **front loops** only, [ch 1, sl st in next st] around.

Fasten off and sew closed.

51. FLOWER

MATERIALS FOR FLOWER

» Yellow yarn (HELLO 122)
» Light blue yarn (HELLO 145)
» 2.5 mm hook
» Two 2 mm black beads & black thread or two 3 mm safety eyes
» Yarn needle
» Pink embroidery floss & needle

With yellow yarn (HELLO 122)

Round 1: Make a magic ring, 6 sc in ring. (6 sc)

Round 2: Inc in each st around. (12 sc)

Round 3: (sc in next st, inc in next st) around. (18 sc)

Round 4: Working in **back loops** only, [dec, sc in next st] around. (12 sc)
If you are using safety eyes, place them in now at Round 2.

Round 5: [Dec] around. (6 sc)
Do not stuff.

Fasten off and sew closed.

Petals
With light blue yarn (HELLO 145)
Join with a slip knot to any front loop of Round 3, ch 1, dc-inc in next front loop, ch 1, [sl st in next front loop, ch 1, dc-inc in next front loop, ch 1] 8 times;

join with sl st to first st. (9 petals)
(photos 1-6)
Fasten off and weave in ends.

Quick Assembly Guide

Eyes: Round 2

Smile: Embroider between eyes at center of flower.

Cheeks: Embroider under eyes

FLOWER ASSEMBLY

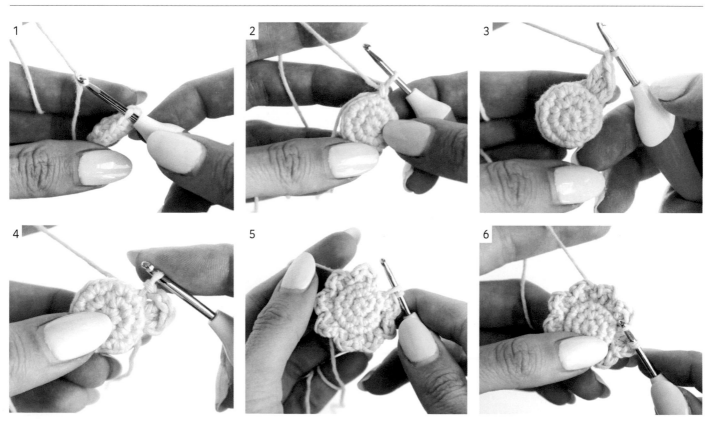

52. MUSHROOM SMALL

MATERIALS FOR MUSHROOM SMALL

» Light beige yarn (HELLO 157)
» Dark beige yarn (HELLO 125)
» 2.5 mm hook
» Two 2 mm black beads & black thread or two 3 mm safety eyes

» Stuffing
» Yarn needle
» Pink embroidery floss & needle

STEM

With light beige yarn (HELLO 157)

Round 1: Make a magic ring, 6 sc in ring. (6 sc)

Rounds 2-6: *(5 rounds)* Sc in each st around. (6 sc)

Round 7: Working in **front loops** only, inc in each st around. (12 sc)

Round 8: [Sc in next st, inc in next st] around. (18 sc)

Fasten off and weave in ends.

CAP

Note: *Make sure you have made the Stem before making the Cap.*

With dark beige yarn (HELLO 125)

Round 1: Make a magic ring, 6 sc in ring. (6 sc)

Round 2: Inc in each st around. (12 sc)

Round 3: [Sc in next st, inc in next st] around. (18 sc)

Round 4: [Sc in each of next 8 sts, inc in next st] around. (20 sc)

Round 5: Sc in each st around. (20 sc) You will now join the Cap to the Stem.

Round 6: Sc around through both pieces (Cap & Stem) using both loops of the cap, but only the **back loop** of the stem. *(photo 1; see note below)*

Note: *The cap has 2 more sts than the stem, so you will need to stitch into 2 of the stem back loops twice. If you are using safety eyes, place them in before closing completely (Round 5, 3 sts apart). Also, stuff the piece before closing completely.*

Fasten off and weave in ends.

53. MUSHROOM BIG

MATERIALS FOR MUSHROOM BIG

» Light beige yarn (HELLO 157)
» Dark beige yarn (HELLO 125)
» 2.5 mm hook
» Two 2 mm black beads & black thread or two 3 mm safety eyes
» Stuffing
» Yarn needle
» Pink embroidery floss & needle

STEM

With light beige yarn (HELLO 157)

Round 1: Make a magic ring, 6 sc in ring. (6 sc)

Rounds 2-6: *(5 rounds)* Sc in each st around. (6 sc)

Round 7: Working in **front loops** only, inc in each st around. (12 sc)

Round 8: [Sc in next st, inc in next st] around. (18 sc)

Round 9: [Sc in each of next 2 sts, inc in next st] around. (24 sc)

Fasten off and weave in ends.

CAP

Note: *Make sure you have made the Stem before making the Cap.*

With dark beige yarn (HELLO 125)

Round 1: Make a magic ring, 6 sc in ring. (6 sc)

Round 2: Inc in each st around. (12 sc)

Round 3: [Sc in next st, inc in next st] around. (18 sc)

Round 4: [Sc in each of next 2 sts, inc in next st] around. (24 sc)

Round 5: [Sc in each of next 11 sts, inc in next st] 2 around. (26 sc)

Round 6: Sc in each st around. (26 sc) You will now join the Cap to the Stem.

Round 7: Sc around through both pieces (Cap & Stem) using both loops of the cap, but only the **back loop** of the stem. *(see note below)*

Note: *The cap has 2 more sts than the stem, so you will need to stitch into 2 of the stem back loops twice. If you are using safety eyes, place them in before closing completely (Round 6, 4 sts apart). Also, stuff the piece before closing completely.*

Fasten off and weave in ends.

COOP

54. ROOSTER
Finished Size
4.5 cm - 1 ¾"

55. CHICKEN
Finished Size
4.5 cm - 1 ¾"

56. LITTLE CHICK
Finished Size
2.5 cm - 1"

57. EGG
Finished Size
2.5 cm - 1"

58. CHICKEN COOP
Finished Size
5.5 cm - 2 ¼"

54. ROOSTER

MATERIALS FOR ROOSTER

» Cinnamon yarn (HELLO 166)
» Light brown yarn (HELLO 167)
» Red yarn (HELLO 113)
» Light green yarn (HELLO 135)
» Dark yellow yarn (HELLO 123)
» 2.5 mm hook

» Two 2mm black beads & black thread or two 3 mm safety eyes
» Stuffing
» Yarn needle
» Pink embroidery floss & needle

BODY & HEAD

With cinnamon yarn (HELLO 166)

Round 1: Make a magic ring, 6 sc in ring. (6 sc)

Round 2: Inc in each st around. (12 sc)

Round 3: [Sc in next st, inc in next st] around. (18 sc)

Rounds 4-6: *(3 rounds)* Sc in each st around. (18 sc)

Change to light brown yarn (HELLO 167)

Round 7: *(Head)* Working in **back loops** only for entire round, sc in each of next 5 sts, skip next 8 sts, sc in each of last 5 sts. (10 sc)

Rounds 8-11: *(4 rounds)* Sc in each st around. (10 sc)

If you are using safety eyes, place them in now at Round 8, 4 sts apart. Stuff.

Round 12: [Dec] around. (5 sc)

Fasten off and sew the head closed.

Stuff the rest of the rooster.

Using some cinnamon yarn, sew the back closed. *(photos 1-3)*

Neck Frill

With light brown yarn (HELLO 167)

Join with a slip knot to any front loop of Round 6, [ch 1, sc in next st, sl st in next st] around.

Fasten off and weave in ends.

WINGS (Make 2)

With light brown yarn (HELLO 167)

Ch 4, (sc, sl st) in 2nd ch from hook, (sl st, ch 1, sc, sl st) in each of next 2 ch, ch 1; working on other side of foundation ch, sc in each of next 3 ch.

Fasten off, leaving a long tail for sewing. *(photo 4)*

COMB

With red yarn (HELLO 113)

Ch 4, (sc, sl st) in 2nd ch from hook, sl st in next ch, (sc, ch 1, sl st) in last ch.

Fasten off, leaving a long tail for sewing.

TAIL (Make 2)

With light green yarn (HELLO 135)

Ch 6, sl st in 2nd ch from hook, sl st in next ch, sc in next ch, sl st in each of last 2 ch.

Fasten off, leaving a long tail for sewing.

LEGS (Make 2)

With dark yellow yarn (HELLO 123)

Ch 5, (sc, sl st) in 2nd ch from hook, sl st in each of next 3 ch.

Fasten off, leaving a long tail for sewing.

BEAK

With dark yellow yarn (HELLO 123)

Ch 2, sc in 2nd ch from hook.

Fasten off, leaving a long tail for sewing.

Quick Assembly Guide

Eyes: Round 8, 4 sts apart
Cheeks: Embroider under eyes
Beak: Sew between eyes
Comb: Round 12, on top of head
Wings: Rounds 4-5, 8 sts apart
Tail: Round 6, at the back
Legs: Rounds 1-2

1

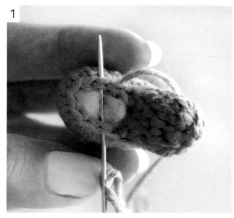

2

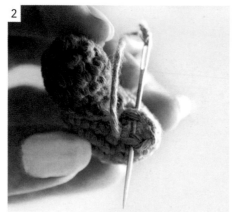

3

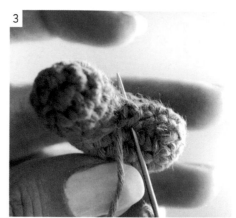

4

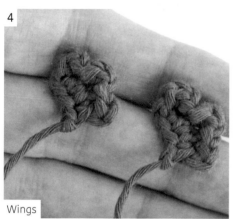

Wings

5

6

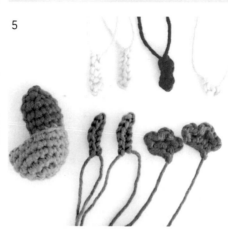

55. CHICKEN

MATERIALS FOR CHICKEN

» Beige yarn (HELLO 157)
» Light beige yarn (HELLO 156)
» Red yarn (HELLO 113)
» Dark yellow yarn (HELLO 123)
» 2.5 mm hook

» Two 2mm black beads & black thread or two 3 mm safety eyes
» Stuffing
» Yarn needle
» Pink embroidery floss & needle

BODY & HEAD

Start with beige yarn (HELLO 157)

Round 1: Make a magic ring, 6 sc in ring. (6 sc)

Round 2: Inc in each st around. (12 sc)

Round 3: [Sc in next st, inc in next st] around. (18 sc)

Rounds 4-6: *(3 rounds)* Sc in each st around. (18 sc)

Change to light beige yarn (HELLO 156)

Round 7: *(Head)* Working in **back loops** only for entire round, sc in each of next 5 sts, skip next 8 sts, sc in each of last 5 sts. (10 sc)

Rounds 8-10: *(3 rounds)* Sc in each st around. (10 sc)

If you are using safety eyes, place them in now at Round 8, 4 sts apart. Stuff.

Round 11: [Dec] around. (5 sc)

Fasten off and sew the head closed.

Stuff the rest of the chicken.

Using some beige yarn, sew the back closed. *(photos 1-2)*

Neck Frill

With light beige yarn (HELLO 156)

Join with a slip knot to any front loop of Round 6, [ch 1, sc in next st, sl st in next st] around.

Fasten off and weave in ends.

WINGS (Make 2)

With beige yarn (HELLO 157)

Ch 4, (sc, sl st) in 2nd ch from hook, (sl st, ch 1, sc, sl st) in each of next 2 ch, ch 1; working on other side of foundation ch, sc in each of next 3 ch.

Fasten off, leaving a long tail for sewing.

COMB

With red yarn (HELLO 113)

Ch 4, (sc, sl st) in 2nd ch from hook, sl st in next ch, (sc, ch 1, sl st) in last ch.

Fasten off, leaving a long tail for sewing.

TAIL

With beige yarn (HELLO 157)

[Ch 3, sl st in 2nd ch from hook, sl st in next ch] 2 times, ch 1, sl st in first st. Fasten off, leaving a long tail for sewing.

LEGS (Make 2)

With dark yellow yarn (HELLO 123)

Ch 5, (sc, sl st) in 2nd ch from hook, sl st in each of next 3 ch.

Fasten off, leaving a long tail for sewing.

BEAK

With dark yellow yarn (HELLO 123)

Ch 2, sc in 2nd ch from hook.

Fasten off, leaving a long tail for sewing.

Quick Assembly Guide

Eyes: Round 8, 4 sts apart

Cheeks: Embroider under eyes

Beak: Sew between eyes

Comb: Round 11, on top of head

Wings: Rounds 4-5, 8 sts apart

Tail: Round 6, at the back

Legs: Rounds 1-2

1

2

3

56. LITTLE CHICK

MATERIALS FOR LITTLE CHICK

- » Yellow yarn (HELLO 123)
- » Orange yarn (HELLO 119)
- » 2.5 mm hook
- » Two 2 mm black beads & black thread or two 3 mm safety eyes
- » Stuffing
- » Yarn needle
- » Pink embroidery floss & needle

With yellow yarn (HELLO 123)

Round 1: Make a magic ring, 6 sc in ring. (6 sc)

Round 2: Inc in each st around. (12 sc)

Rounds 3-4: *(2 rounds)* Sc in each st around. (12 sc)

Round 5: Inc in each of next 2 sts, sc in each of next 10 sts. (14 sc)

Round 6: [Sc in next st, inc in next st] 2 times, sc in each of next 10 sts. (16 sc)

If you are using safety eyes, place them in now after the 9th and 12th sts of Round 5 (2 sts apart).

Round 7: Sc in each st around. (16 sc)

Round 8: [Dec] 2 times, [sc in next st, dec] 4 times. (10 sc)

Stuff.

Round 9: [Dec] around. (5 sc)

Fasten off and sew closed.

WINGS (Make 2)

With yellow yarn (HELLO 123)

Ch 2, (hdc, ch 1, sl st) in 2nd ch from hook.

Fasten off, leaving a long tail for sewing.

Embroidering Details

With orange yarn (HELLO 119), embroider 2 straight stitches between the eyes as a beak and 2 straight stitches for each leg under each eye.

Quick Assembly Guide

Eyes: Round 5, 2 sts apart

Beak: Embroider between eyes.

Cheeks: Embroider under eyes.

Wings: Round 5, 6 sts apart.

Legs: Embroider at Rounds 6-7, under each eye

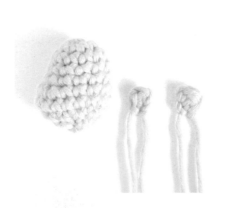

57. EGG

MATERIALS FOR EGG

» Light beige yarn (HELLO 156)

» 2.5 mm hook

» Stuffing

» Yarn needle

With light beige yarn (HELLO 156)

Round 1: Make a magic ring, 4 sc in ring. (4 sc)

Round 2: Inc in each st around. (8 sc)

Round 3: [Sc in next st, inc in next st] around. (12 sc)

Rounds 4-7: *(4 rounds)* Sc in each st around. (12 sc)

Stuff.

Round 8: [Dec] around. (6 sc)
Fasten off and sew closed.

58. CHICKEN COOP

MATERIALS FOR CHICKEN COOP

» Beige yarn (HELLO 125)
» Red yarn (HELLO 113)
» 2.5 mm hook
» Yarn needle

PIECE 1

With beige yarn (HELLO 125)

Note: *Refer to photo 1 (P. 111) and Diagram 3 (P. 113) when making Piece 1. You start with the center (1-Y in Diagram 3) and then make three walls (1-W, 1-X, and 1-Z in Diagram 3). Finally, you make the Beam that will support the roof across the front of the coop.*

Round 1: Make a magic ring, 8 sc in ring. (8 sc)

Round 2: [Sc in next st, (3 sc) in next st] around. (16 sc)

Round 3: Sc in each of next 2 sts, (3 sc) in next st, [sc in each of next 3 sts, (3 sc) in next st] 3 times, sc in last st. (24 sc)

Round 4: Sc in each of next 3 sts, (3 sc) in next st, [sc in each of next 5 sts, (3 sc) in next st] 3 times, sc in each of last 2 sts. (32 sc)

Round 5: Sc in each of next 4 sts, (3 sc) in next st, [sc in each of next 7 sts, (3 sc) in next st] 3 times, sc in each of last 3 sts. (40 sc)

Fasten off and weave in ends.

Next, you will be adding walls to 3 sides of the square you just made. *(photo 1)*

Row 1: Working in **back loops** only, join with a sc in a corner stitch, sc in each of next 9 sts. (10 sc)

Rows 2-13: *(12 rows)* Ch 1, turn, sc in each of next 10 sts. (10 sc)

Fasten off, leaving a long tail for sewing.

Repeat Rows 1-13 for two more sides, but when you reach the end of the last piece, don't fasten off, but continue on to make the Beam.

(Beam) Ch 11, sc in 2nd ch from hook, sc in each of next 9 ch. (10 sc) *(photo 1)*

Fasten off, leaving a long tail for sewing.

PIECE 2

With beige yarn (HELLO 125)

Round 1: Make a magic ring, 8 sc in ring. (8 sc)

Round 2: [Sc in next st, (3 sc) in next st] around. (16 sc)

Round 3: Sc in each of next 2 sts, (3 sc) in next st, [sc in each of next 3 sts, (3 sc) in next st] 3 times, sc in last st (24 sc)

Round 4: Sc in each of next 3 sts, (3 sc) in next st, [sc in each of next 5 sts, (3 sc) in next st] 3 times, sc in each of last 2 sts. (32 sc)

Round 5: Sc in each of next 4 sts, (3 sc) in next st, [sc in each of next 7 sts, (3 sc) in next st] 3 times, sc in each of last 3 sts. (40 sc)

Fasten off and weave in ends. *(photo 2, far left piece)*

PIECES 3 & 4

With beige yarn (HELLO 125)

Follow Rows 1-10 twice to make two identical pieces (Pieces 3 and 4).

Row 1: Ch 12, sc in 2nd ch from hook, sc in each of next 10 ch. (11 sc)

Rows 2-10: *(9 rows)* Ch 1, turn, sc in each of next 11 sts. (11 sc)

Fasten off, leaving a long tail for sewing.
(photo 2, two pieces on right)

ROOF

With red yarn (HELLO 113)

Row 1: Ch 15, hdc in 3rd ch from hook, hdc in each of next 12 ch. (13 hdc)

Row 2: Working in **back loops** only, ch 2, turn, hdc in each st across. (13 hdc)

Row 3: Working in **front loops** only ch 2, turn, hdc in each st across. (13 hdc)

Row 4: Working in **back loops** only, ch 2, turn, hdc in each st across. (13 hdc)

Row 5: Working in **front loops** only ch 2, turn, hdc in each st across. (13 hdc)

Row 6: Working in **back loops** only, ch 2, turn, hdc in each st across. (13 hdc)

Row 7: Working in **front loops** only, ch 2, turn, hdc in each st across. (13 hdc)

Make (2 hdc) in same stitch as last hdc.

Rotate the piece; you will now work in the sides of the rows.

Sl st in next row, [(3 hdc) in next row, sl st in next row] 3 times.

Fasten off, leaving a long tail for sewing. *(photo 3)*

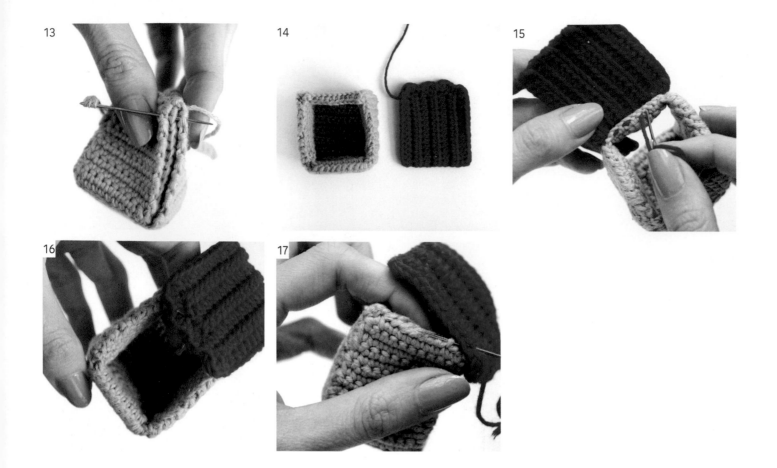

CHICKEN COOP

COOP ASSEMBLY INSTRUCTIONS

Attaching Pieces 2, 3, and 4 Together

Sew one side of Piece 3 onto one side of Piece 2, using only the **front loops** of Piece 2 and the sides of the rows of piece 3. *(photos 4-6 and diagrams 1-2)*

Sew the pieces so they create a right angle (Piece 3 is vertical).

Repeat the same for Piece 4, on the opposite side of Piece 2, to create a U shaped piece.

Diagram 1

Diagram 2

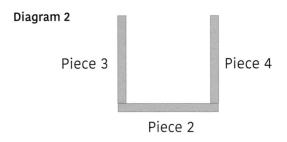

Attaching to Piece 1

Place the 3-part piece (2, 3, and 4 combined) on top of Piece 1 (over 1-X, 1-Y, and 1-Z) and sew the two layers together. Referring to Diagram 4, start on side A and continue to side B *(Diagram 4, photos 7-9)*.

Diagram 3

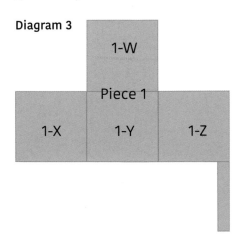

Diagram 4

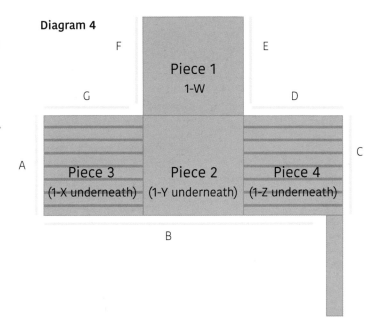

After sewing the bottom side (B), sew the base of the beam to the end of side B to secure it in place. *(photos 10-11)*

Continue sewing Piece 1-Z and Piece 4 together along side C.

The last sides (D to G) will be sewn a bit differently. Fold the top part of Piece 1 (1-W) down and sew its side E together with side D of both Piece 4 and Piece 1-Z, sewing through all three layers. *(photos 12-13)*

Repeat for sides F and G, sewing through all three layers again (side F of Piece 1-W, and side G of both Piece 3 and Piece 1-X).

Attach the free end of the beam to the opposite side of the coop (at the corner of sides A and B).

Attaching the Roof

Start sewing the roof onto the top of the coop by attaching the front -wavy- part onto the beam, then continue on to the other sides, all the way around. *(photos 15-17)*

Animals

59. CAT
Finished Size
5.5 cm - 2 ¼"

60. DOG
Finished Size
5.5 cm - 2 ¼"

61. MONKEY
Finished Size
5.5 cm - 2 ¼"

62. MOUSE
Finished Size
6 cm - 2 ½"

59. CAT

MATERIALS FOR CAT

» Gray yarn (HELLO 174)
» Dark gray yarn (HELLO 159)
» White yarn (HELLO 155)
» 2.5 mm hook
» Two 2 mm black beads & black

thread or two 3 mm safety eyes
» Stuffing
» Yarn needle
» Pink embroidery floss & needle

BODY

With gray yarn (HELLO 174)

Round 1: Ch 4, sc in 2nd ch from hook, sc in next ch, inc in last ch; working on other side of foundation ch, sc in each of next 2 ch, inc in last ch. (8 sc)

Round 2: [Inc in next st, sc in next st] around. (12 sc)

Round 3: Sc in next st, [inc in next st, sc in each of next 2 sts] 3 times, inc in next st, sc in next st. (16 sc)

Rounds 4-11: *(8 rounds)* Sc in each st around. (16 sc)

If you are using safety eyes, place them in now at Round 6, 4 sts apart.

Round 12: [Dec, sc in each of next 2 sts] around. (12 sc)

Stuff.

Round 13: [Dec] around. (6 sc)

Fasten off and sew closed.

ARMS & LEGS (Make 4)

With gray yarn (HELLO 174)

Row 1: Ch 5, sc in 2nd ch from hook, sc in each of next 3 ch. (4 sc)

Row 2: Ch 1, turn, sc in each of next 4 sts. (4 sc)

Fasten off, leaving a long tail for sewing.

Sew along the long edges (whipstitch) to form a long cylinder. *(photos 1-3)*

EARS (Make 2)

With gray yarn (HELLO 174)

Round 1: Make a magic ring, 4 sc in ring. (4 sc)

Round 2: Inc in next st, sc in each of next 3 sts. (5 sc)

Round 3: [Inc in next st, sc in next st] 2 times, inc in last st. (8 sc)

Do not stuff. Fasten off, leaving a long tail for sewing.

BELLY

With white yarn (HELLO 155)

Round 1: Ch 4, sc in 2nd ch from hook, sc in next ch, inc in last ch; working on other side of foundation ch, sc in each of next 2 ch, inc in last ch. (8 sc)

Round 2: [Inc in next st, sc in next st] around. (12 sc)

Fasten off, leaving a long tail for sewing.

TAIL

With gray yarn (HELLO 174)

Ch 10, sc in 2nd ch from hook, sc in each of next 8 ch. (9 sc)

Fasten off, leaving a long tail for sewing.

Sew along the long edges (whipstitch) to form a long cylinder. *(photos 4-6)*

Embroidering Details

With dark grey yarn (HELLO 159), embroider 3 straight stitches on top of the head.

Quick Assembly Guide

Eyes: Round 6, 4 sts apart
Cheeks: Embroider under eyes
Nose: Embroider between eyes
Ears: Rounds 1-2, on the sides
Arms: Rounds 7-8, 7 sts apart
Legs: Round 12, 2 sts apart
Tail: Rounds 9-10

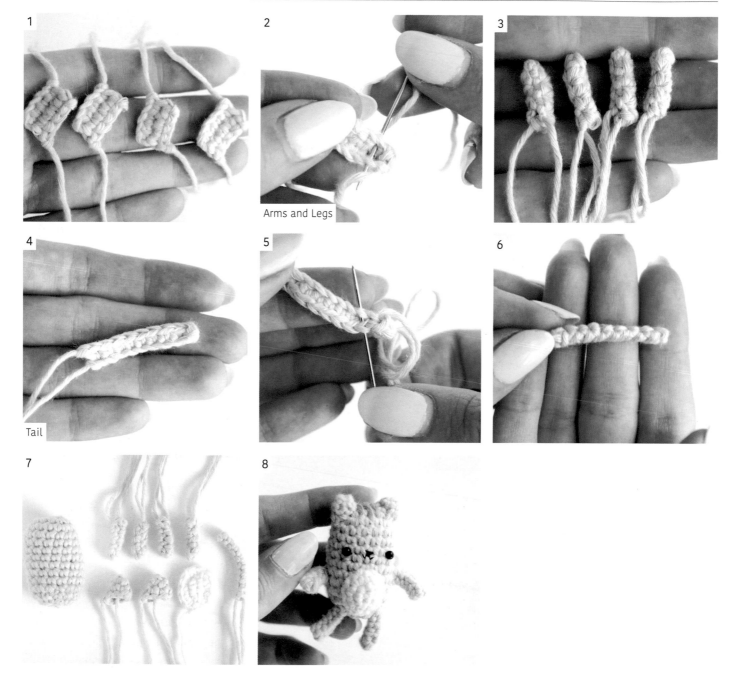

1

2

Arms and Legs

3

4

Tail

5

6

7

8

60. DOG

MATERIALS FOR DOG

» Cinnamon yarn (HELLO 166)
» Black yarn (HELLO 160)
» White yarn (HELLO 155)
» 2.5 mm hook

» Two 2 mm black beads & black thread or two 3 mm safety eyes
» Stuffing
» Yarn needle
» Pink embroidery floss & needle

BODY

With cinnamon yarn (HELLO 166)

Round 1: Ch 4, sc in 2nd ch from hook, sc in next ch, inc in last ch; working on other side of foundation ch, sc in each of next 2 ch, inc in last ch. (8 sc)

Round 2: [Inc in next st, sc in next st] around.
(12 sc)

Round 3: Sc in next st, [inc in next st, sc in each of next 2 sts] 3 times, inc in next st, sc in next st. (16 sc)

Rounds 4-11: *(8 rounds)* Sc in each st around. (16 sc)

If you are using safety eyes, place them in now at Round 6, 4 sts apart.

Round 12: [Dec, sc in each of next 2 sts] around. (12 sc)

Stuff.

Round 13: [Dec] around. (6 sc)

Fasten off and sew closed.

ARMS & LEGS (Make 4)

With cinnamon yarn (HELLO 166)

Row 1: Ch 5, sc in 2nd ch from hook, sc in each of next 3 ch. (4 sc)

Row 2: Ch 1, turn, sc in each of next 4 sts. (4 sc)

Fasten off, leaving a long tail for sewing.

Sew along the long edges (whipstitch) to form a long cylinder.

EARS (Make 2)

With black yarn (HELLO 160)

Round 1: Make a magic ring, 5 sc in ring. (5 sc)

Rounds 2-3: *(2 rounds)* Sc in each st around. (5 sc)

Round 4: Sc in each of next 3 sts; end round here. (3 sc)

Do not stuff.

Fasten off, leaving a long tail for sewing.

TAIL

With cinnamon yarn (HELLO 166)

Row 1: Ch 4, sc in 2nd ch from hook, sc in each of next 2 ch. (3 sc)

Row 2: Ch 1, turn, sc in next st, sl st in each of next 2 sts. (1 sc & 2 sl st)

Fasten off, leaving a long tail for sewing.

Sew along the long edges (whipstitch) to form a long cylinder.

BELLY

With white yarn (HELLO 155)

Round 1: Ch 4, sc in 2nd ch from hook, sc in next ch, inc in last ch; working on other side of foundation ch, sc in each of next 2 ch, inc in last ch. (8 sc)

Round 2: [Inc in next st, sc in next st] around. (12 sc)

Fasten off, leaving a long tail for sewing.

Quick Assembly Guide

Eyes: Round 6, 4 sts apart
Cheeks: Embroider under eyes
Nose: Embroider between eyes
Ears: Rounds 1-2, on the sides
Arms: Rounds 7-8, 7 sts apart
Legs: Round 12, 2 sts apart
Tail: Rounds 9-10

62. MOUSE

MATERIALS FOR MOUSE

» Gray yarn (HELLO 174)

» 2.5 mm hook

» Two 2 mm black beads & black thread or two 3 mm safety eyes

» Stuffing

» Yarn needle

» Pink embroidery floss & needle

BODY

With gray yarn (HELLO 174)

Round 1: Ch 4, sc in 2nd ch from hook, sc in next ch, inc in last ch; working on other side of foundation ch, sc in each of next 2 ch, inc in last ch. (8 sc)

Round 2: [Inc in next st, sc in next st] around. (12 sc)

Round 3: Sc in next st, [inc in next st, sc in each of next 2 sts] 3 times, inc in next st, sc in next st. (16 sc)

Rounds 4-11: *(8 rounds)* Sc in each st around. (16 sc)

If you are using safety eyes, place them in now at Round 6, 4 sts apart.

Round 12: [Dec, sc in each of next 2 sts] around. (12 sc)

Stuff.

Round 13: [Dec] around. (6 sc)

Fasten off and sew closed.

ARMS & LEGS (Make 4)

With gray yarn (HELLO 174)

Row 1: Ch 5, sc in 2nd ch from hook, sc in each of next 3 ch. (4 sc)

Row 2: Ch 1, turn, sc in each of next 4 sts. (4 sc)

Fasten off, leaving a long tail for sewing.

Sew along the long edges (whipstitch) to form a long cylinder.

EARS

With gray yarn (HELLO 174)

Round 1: Make a magic ring, 6 sc in ring. (6 sc)

Round 2: Inc in each of next 4 sts, sl st in each of last 2 sts. (8 sc & 2 sl st)

Fasten off, leaving a long tail for sewing.

When attaching the ears on the head (at Rounds 2-4 of body), sew through the last 2 sl sts of each ear.

Quick Assembly Guide

Eyes: Round 6, 4 sts apart

Cheeks: Embroider under eyes

Nose: Embroider between eyes

Ears: Rounds 2-5, on the sides

Arms: Rounds 9-10, 7 sts apart

Legs: Round 12, 2 sts apart

61. MONKEY

MATERIALS FOR MONKEY

» Brown yarn (HELLO 167)
» Pale peach yarn (HELLO 162)
» 2.5 mm hook
» Two 2 mm black beads & black thread or two 3 mm safety eyes
» Stuffing
» Yarn needle
» Pink embroidery floss & needle

BODY

With brown yarn (HELLO 167)

Round 1: Ch 4, sc in 2nd ch from hook, sc in next ch, inc in last ch; working on other side of foundation ch, sc in each of next 2 ch, inc in last ch. (8 sc)

Round 2: [Inc in next st, sc in next st] around. (12 sc)

Round 3: Sc in next st, [inc in next st, sc in each of next 2 sts] 3 times, inc in next st, sc in next st. (16 sc)

Rounds 4-11: *(8 rounds)* Sc in each st around. (16 sc)

If you are using safety eyes, place them in now at Round 5, 4 sts apart.

Round 12: [Dec, sc in each of next 2 sts] around. (12 sc)

Stuff.

Round 13: [Dec] around. (6 sc)

Fasten off and sew closed.

ARMS & LEGS (Make 4)

With brown yarn (HELLO 167)

Row 1: Ch 5, sc in 2nd ch from hook, sc in each of next 3 ch. (4 sc)

Row 2: Ch 1, turn, sc in each of next 4 sts. (4 sc)

Fasten off, leaving a long tail for sewing.

Sew along the long edges (whipstitch) to form a long cylinder.

EARS (MAKE 2)

With brown yarn (HELLO 167)

Round 1: Make a magic ring, 6 sc in ring. (6 sc)

Round 2: [Sc in next st, inc in next st] around. (9 sc)

Round 3: Sc in each st around. (9 sc)

Fasten off, leaving a long tail for sewing. Do not stuff.

TAIL

With brown yarn (HELLO 167)

Ch 9, sc in 2nd ch from hook, sc in each of next 7 ch. (8 sc)

Fasten off, leaving a long tail for sewing.

Sew along the long edges (whipstitch) to form a long cylinder.

MUZZLE

With pale peach yarn (HELLO 162)

Round 1: Ch 5, sc in 2nd ch from hook, sc in each of next 2 ch, inc in last ch; working on other side of foundation ch, sc in each of next 3 ch, inc in last ch. (10 sc)

Round 2: Sc in each st around. (10 sc)

Fasten off, leaving a long tail for sewing. Lightly stuff.

Quick Assembly Guide

Eyes: Round 5, 4 sts apart
Cheeks: Embroider under eyes
Nostrils: Embroider on muzzle
Smile: Embroider on muzzle
Ears: Rounds 3-7, on the sides
Arms: Rounds 9-10, 7 sts apart
Legs: Round 12, 2 sts apart
Tail: Rounds 9-10

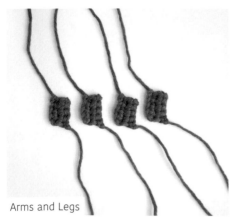

Arms and Legs

Ears